YOU
ARE
CREATIVE,
U
JUST
DON'T
KNOW
IT
YET.

EMERGE

BY DON PERINI

pot-boilers

All Scripture quotations, unless otherwise indicated, are taken from the Holy Bible, New International Version, NIV. Copyright © 1973, 1978, 1984 by Biblica, Inc. TM used by permission of Zondervan. All rights reserved worldwide www.zondervan.com

Requests for permission should be made in writing to:
Pot-Boilers, 100 Stevens St. SW, Grand Rapids, MI 49507

Copyright © 2014
by Don Perini

WWW.POT-BOILERS.COM

Book jacket
design &
layout
by Deksia
Design LLC.

ISBN 9780-578-13514-490000

Manufactured in the
United States of America
1 2 3 56 78 23 23 11

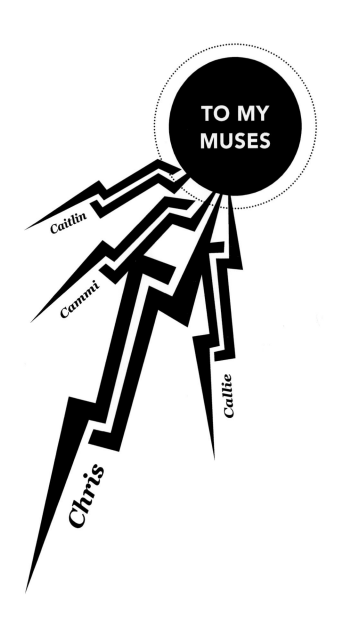

TO MY
MUSES

Caitlin

Cammi

Callie

Chris

IF YOU WANT A QUICK FIX, PUT THIS BOOK DOWN!

If you are looking for a fast and easy way to unleash your creative potential, then this book, I am sorry to say, is not for you. If you desire to develop creative habits without much effort, or you are seeking a simple formula that will develop your unique talents, you will be disappointed to learn that I have nothing to teach you. I don't believe in the existence of a single formula or a step-by-step process for cultivating creativity.

While a few individuals have accomplished their creative endeavors with ease, they are the exception rather than the norm. I guess that makes me normal. Most individuals—99.9%—have seen their creative endeavors come to fruition at the cost of much time, effort, and pain.

ARE YOU SURE YOU STILL WANT TO DO THIS?

A creative person is well-trained. I'll say it again: A creative person is well-trained. Creativity is not done on the fly—it takes discipline and hard work. If you are willing to change your lifestyle, work hard to develop creative habits, and delve deeply into the darkest part of your soul, then this book is for you. This book is a guide, not a formula, to help you with your quest to live a creative life.

I don't claim that this book is exhaustive on the topic of creativity. The creative habits mentioned here are common practices that I have found through my research. But whether you are a writer, homemaker, artist, engineer, scientist, inventor, entrepreneur, pastor, scholar, or musician, I welcome you on a journey that will change your life forever.

It changed mine.

IN
TRO
_02

WE
HAVE
ACCESS

I enjoy being a professor of creativity, but there are times when it can be downright dreadful. Imagine being in a square room with a large table at the center. A well-dressed, confident woman is leading the meeting with twelve of her colleagues, including myself. She clearly states the problem and asks the group with a smile, "What ideas do you have?"

An uncomfortable silence takes over as everyone tries to avoid eye contact with the presenter. Some don't want to be chosen because they feel they don't have a good answer. Others just don't care about the discussion. As the awkward silence continues, the tension grows. I begin to sweat and hope my deodorant will live up to its claims. I know what is about to happen. It happens every time. The leader attempts to make eye contact with me as I repeat over and over in my mind, "Don't pick me!" Mind over matter doesn't work. It never does. The leader regains her confidence and says those dreaded words that I hear so often, "Perini, you're a professor of creativity. What ideas do you have?"

Don't they know creativity doesn't work like that? They expect that I can conjure up a great solution in a matter of moments. It's an impossible expectation and one that I cannot meet. So I sit back in my chair and respond, "I got nothing."

Everyone in the room is disappointed. After all, shouldn't the professor of creativity always have a solution? You can imagine what it's like when I give the same answer time after time. My colleagues begin to wonder who this professor is and whether he's any good at what he does. I can feel their lack of confidence in me grow. What they don't understand is that creativity isn't a genie in a bottle. It takes determination, process, and good habits to come up with great results.

Recently I was up for a sabbatical. I didn't hesitate to fill out the appropriate forms, since this was my chance to avoid those awkward and dreadful meetings. I was finally free from looking like I didn't know what I was doing.

I did what most professors do while sabbaticalling. (New word! Maybe I'm creative after all.) I went down to my basement, surrounded myself with books, and began to read. My goal was to write a book on creativity-one that addressed the topic from a theological, philosophical, and psychological point of view, but that was also very practical to the reader. During my studies several questions emerged, ones that would shape the contents of this book.

? Why do some teachers do a better job of teaching than their peers?

? Why do some athletes outperform other athletes with similar talents?

? Why do certain scientists, entrepreneurs, architects, and writers rise above the crowd?

? What did Leonardo da Vinci, Thomas Edison, Salvador Dali, and Winston Churchill have in common?

Are highly successful people born that way? Are they just smarter than most of us? If so, I am in trouble. I can't measure up to these characters. But there is good news. As I continued to do my research, I discovered something truly amazing and profound.

WE ALL HAVE ACCESS TO WHAT THEY ARE DOING.

BY READING THIS BOOK YOU
WILL LEARN WHAT OTHER
CREATIVE PEOPLE HAVE DONE
TO ACHIEVE GREAT RESULTS AND
FIND AMAZING SUCCESS. USING
A PHILOSOPHICAL FRAMEWORK
I CALL CREATIVE EMERGENCE, A
BIBLICAL VIEW OF HUMANITY, AND
AN EXAMINATION OF CREATIVE
HABITS, YOU WILL DISCOVER HOW
TO UNLEASH YOUR POTENTIAL,
GROW YOUR TALENTS, THRIVE IN
YOUR CAREER, AND COMPLETE
YOUR CREATIVE ENDEAVORS. IN
THE END I WANT THE PRACTICE OF
CREATIVE EMERGENCE TO CHANGE
YOUR LIFE FOR THE BETTER. YOU
WILL BE ABLE TO SHOUT WITH
CONFIDENCE, **"I AM CREATIVE!"**

WHAT
IS
CREATIVE?

3

Three introductions in one book—that's a new one. But does that make it creative? I often hear people use the term "creative" for anything that is novel or original. But that is really only half the story.

Creatologists (another new word!) are those who study the subject of creativity. They define creativity as works that are both new and useful. Having three introductions is new. I have not seen it done before. But is it useful? I will let you decide that and determine whether my third introduction is creative by being both new and useful.

IN
TRO
_04

BECAUSE
I CAN

Now let's get on
with the book.
SHALL WE?

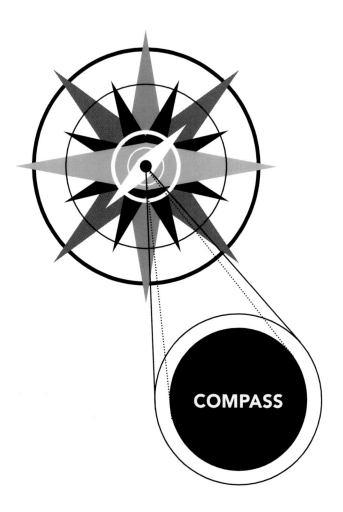

COMPASS

FULLY
HUMAN

"IN THE
BEGINNING
GENESIS 1:1

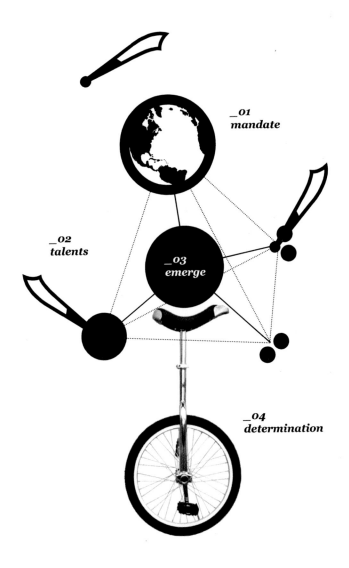

_01
mandate

_02
talents

_03
emerge

_04
determination

MANDATE

BE FRUITFUL & MULTIPLY & FILL THE EARTH & SUBDUE IT.
GENESIS 1:28

Imagine it is Christmas morning and you are seven years old. You wait at the top of the stairs as your parents prepare the living room for the celebration. You squirm, fuss, and protest, wondering why your parents move at a turtle's pace. The anticipation is unbearable. After what seems like an eternity, you are finally given permission to come down and unleash your world-renowned unwrapping talents. Three stairs at a time, you rush down to see what is under the tree. But then you stop as if you've hit a wall, because right before your eyes is the greatest gift ever.

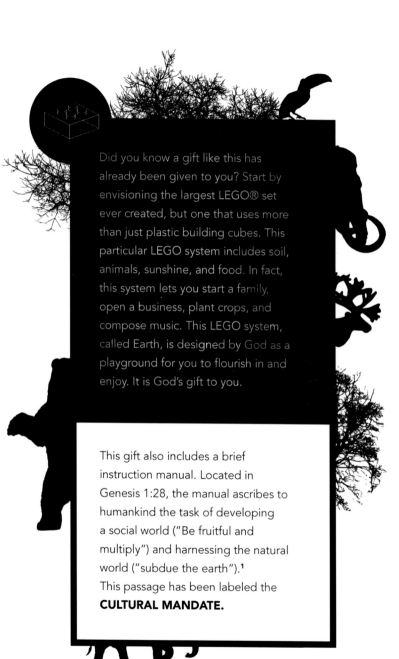

Did you know a gift like this has already been given to you? Start by envisioning the largest LEGO® set ever created, but one that uses more than just plastic building cubes. This particular LEGO system includes soil, animals, sunshine, and food. In fact, this system lets you start a family, open a business, plant crops, and compose music. This LEGO system, called Earth, is designed by God as a playground for you to flourish in and enjoy. It is God's gift to you.

This gift also includes a brief instruction manual. Located in Genesis 1:28, the manual ascribes to humankind the task of developing a social world ("Be fruitful and multiply") and harnessing the natural world ("subdue the earth").[1]
This passage has been labeled the **CULTURAL MANDATE.**

Like most instruction manuals, it also comes with a warning. You may recall the whole tree and apple story in which God told Adam and Eve, "Don't eat this." Well, they did. And thanks to the first couple, our beautiful LEGO system is no longer in its original state.

But just because Adam and Eve didn't heed the warning label doesn't mean the cultural mandate given in Genesis 1 changed. We are still supposed to develop a social world, and we are called to harness the natural world. But since sin has entered this world, our creative endeavors have the tendency to become immoral. Let us not forget the Tower of Babel story found in Genesis 11:1-9, where humankind "wanted to make a name for itself" and did not want to "be scattered over the face of the whole earth." Their brand of culture making,[2] the building of the tower, was an offense to God; as a result, He gave them different languages and scattered them all over the earth.

SO THE LESSON HERE IS SIMPLE...
When you embark on fulfilling the Cultural Mandate, whether it be gardening, writing, entrepreneuring (okay—that new word is a little awkward), or designing, it must be done in a way that pleases and glorifies God.

YOUR ENDEAVORS MAY NOT:

1_Dismiss God
2_Elevate humanity above God.

If they do, they become immoral.

At the core of our immoral behavior is an attempt to find personal worth, just as it was with the builders of Babel. Like them, we believe the best way to achieve personal worth is by gaining significance and obtaining security. But the world and our efforts alone can never completely satisfy our need for personal worth. Think about the slogan from candy company Mars, Inc., which boasts that their Snickers® candy bar, filled with nougat, caramel, peanuts, and milk chocolate, will "satisfy" your needs. Sure, it satisfies your appetite. Sure, it satisfies your chocolate cravings. Sure, it satisfies your depleted energy...but only for a short while. Eventually you will get hungry again, and you will need something more substantial.

Your own efforts to find personal worth are always temporary. They give the illusion that significance and security can be found through fame and fortune. But the truth is this: your personal worth can only be "satisfied" when you discover what it means to be fully human. To be fully human means to live a life that glorifies God by pursuing creative endeavors as acts of worship. Our actions should bring the Kingdom of God ("thy Kingdom come," as we pray in The Lord's Prayer) here to earth so the world can see the glory of God now in the present. Fortunately, when we "fall short" we still belong to God, no matter what. We are significant, as image bearers, and secure, because of His unconditional love. There is nothing you can do to earn this love and acceptance. It is free.

IF WE ARE TO FOLLOW
THE CULTURAL MANDATE
APPROPRIATELY, THAT IS, BY
DEVELOPING A SOCIAL WORLD
AND HARNESSING THE NATURAL
WORLD, THEN WE NEED TO
EXAMINE OUR HEARTS. WE
NEED TO RID THEM OF THE
DESIRE TO ELEVATE OUR NAMES
ABOVE HIS AND/OR DISMISS
GOD IN AN EFFORT TO FIND
PERSONAL WORTH. SO LET US
FULFILL THE CULTURAL MANDATE
BY STARTING WITH PURE AND
CLEAN HEARTS. LET US BUILD
FAMILIES, WRITE STORIES, AND
CREATE BUSINESSES FOR THE
PURPOSE OF ADVANCING GOD'S
KINGDOM, NOT OUR OWN.

IT IS OUR MANDATE.

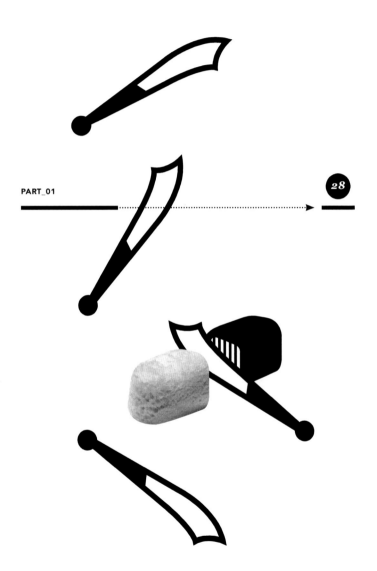

TALENT

"THE IMAGE OF GOD IS A TASK, A MISSION."
JAMES K. A. SMITH

In ancient Rome there was an architectural feature called the Vomitorium. Do you know what purpose it served? At first glance, you would think it was a room where the Romans could purge rotten food with some privacy. But you would be wrong. Rather, it was an entryway, below a tier of seats, where large crowds could enter and exit a stadium. Hold that thought for a second.

We all have misconceptions about reality. Take for example the myth that we swallow an average of eight spiders per year while we sleep, or the one about Twinkies having an indefinite shelf life. Both of these "facts" are simply not true.

I have had many misconceptions of my own. In Genesis 1:26 we are given a very brief description of humanity. It reads, "Then God said, 'Let us make human beings in our image, in our likeness, so that they may rule...'". Throughout history Christians have used the term imago Dei, Latin for "image of God," to depict this reality.

My misconception about imago Dei came from the word "likeness" found in the middle of this passage. I read it and thought, "Oh, this must mean I am somewhat like Him in being or essence." I couldn't have been further from the truth. I was making the same mistake you may have made with the word vomitorium by thinking it had something to do with the word "vomit".

Imago Dei is not a description of our being, like a soul, or a mind, or a hand. Don't forget that Jesus Christ is the only incarnation of God in human form. Rather, we are like Him in our tasks. In other words, imago Dei is a mission.

Richard Middleton, in *The Liberating Image*, explains this well. "The imago Dei designates the royal office or calling of human beings as God's representatives and agents in the world, granted authorized power to share in God's rule or administration of the earth's resources and creatures."

Middleton, J. Richard. The Liberating Image: The Image Dei in Genesis 1. Grand Rapids, MI: Brazos, 2005. Print

To better understand this idea of image-bearing, it may help to see how it was applied in the Ancient Near East. Ancient rulers would place statues of themselves in cities throughout their kingdom. These statues or images were placed as reminders of who was ruling over them and who was to be worshipped and followed. Likewise, we are God's image bearers in this world, reflecting the glory of God here. As image bearers, we are to wisely rule, as God rules, when we carry out the Cultural Mandate. This is our vocation and mission as Christ-followers.

But we are not left to our own devices to accomplish this task. God provides each of us with a set of talents to carry out His mandate. These talents are freely given, and they cannot be earned. Since they are free, many have ascribed another term for them. They call them 'gifts'.

I thought about coming up with a new word to describe this truth that talents are free gifts given to us by God.

GIFTS + TALENTS = GALENTS

TALENTS + GIFTS = TIFTS

But galents or tifts just doesn't quite do the trick.

I should stop here and address a question many of you may want to ask. What are the similarities and differences between talents and spiritual gifts? The similarities are that they are both freely given by God and can develop and grow in effectiveness. But the difference between them is this: Spiritual gifts are given by the Holy Spirit to do "works of service" for the Church (Ephesians 4:12), whereas talents, though they can also be used to serve others, are primarily for culture-making.

If we are to share our rule with God (imago Dei) and fulfill our task of culture making (Cultural Mandate), it seems clear that we need to develop our talents. Talent development should bring joy and pleasure to our lives, as it is part of the experience and intended purpose that comes with this playground called Earth. Unfortunately, many distractions keep us from developing our talents. These distractions will be addressed later in this book.

SO, HOW DO WE DEVELOP OUR TALENTS?

Before I answer that question, I would like to make a few brief points regarding talents. First, you must never compare your talents with those of other individuals. This will only lead to envy and discouragement and prevent you from fulfilling your dreams. Just don't go there. Second, if you want to master your talents, you must develop and grow them. If you don't put in the time, energy, and effort needed for your talents to develop, they will atrophy. Third, God has made you unique, with your own set of talents. There is no one else like you. Accept yourself as you are. You are enough. Fourth, each of us has varying degrees of talents. Think about each talent having a proficiency rating between one and ten. You might be able to reach level two with one talent, while with another you can reach level nine. It is perfectly normal that most of your talents would be at a medium to low level. You will want to focus on those high-level talents God has given you, not on the ones you don't have. Focus on your strengths.

Now back to our question. How can you develop your talents? I would suggest that living the creative life, which involves practicing creative habits, is the best way to achieve this. By combining your talents with creative habits, you will increase your talents' effectiveness, and something amazing **will** emerge. I call this phenomenon "creative emergence," and it is how culture-making occurs.

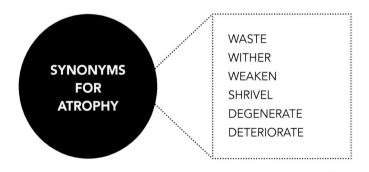

SYNONYMS FOR ATROPHY

WASTE
WITHER
WEAKEN
SHRIVEL
DEGENERATE
DETERIORATE

TALENT IN A DOMAIN

Jane Piirto has done extensive studies on talent development and how it shapes the lives of creative people. She contends that Home, School, Gender, Community/Culture, and Chance are the five most important environmental factors which play a significant role in the talent development of Creatives. Furthermore, she suggests that your "calling" is tied to your unique talents.

ART	**MUSIC**
VISUAL	**THEATRE**
SCIENCE	**WRITING**
BUSINESS	**ATHLETICS**
MATH	**DANCE**
SPIRITUAL	**INVENTION**
ACADEMICS	**MECHANICAL**
INTERPERSONAL	**ENTREPRENEURIAL**

"EMERGENCE IS THE PROCESS OF CONSTITUTING A NEW REALITY WITH ITS OWN PARTICULAR CHARACTERISTICS THROUGH THE INTERACTIVE COMBINATION OF OTHER, DIFFERENT ENTITIES THAT ARE NECESSARY TO CREATE THE NEW ENTITY BUT THAT DO NOT CONTAIN THE CHARACTERISTICS PRESENT IN THE NEW ENTITY."

CHRISTIAN SMITH

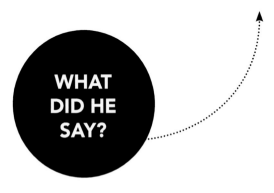

WHAT
DID HE
SAY?

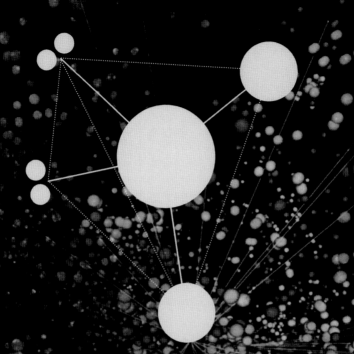

EMERGE

What emerges when you combine hydrogen and oxygen? A new entity called water. And if you combine metal, silicon, electrical energy, and various other materials in just the right way, you can create a computer. On the other hand, when you combine high fructose corn syrup, vegetable shortening, enriched wheat flour, niacin, yellow #5, and other harmful ingredients together, you get something called a Twinkie. This philosophical reality is called emergence. It happens all the time, for good and for bad.

But some do not believe that an entity can be greater than the sum of its parts. They want to interpret the world at its lowest level, a philosophical idea called reductionism. This theory asserts that the human body is **nothing but** cells, fluids, hydrogen, sulfur, and carbon dioxide.

Before I launch into a critical analysis of Reductionism, I would like to suggest that this view is very helpful if you are trying to answer questions like "What is this made of?" or "How does this work?". If you want to better understand the human heart or a tree or a computer, one of the best ways to do it is to break the item down into its smallest parts. A reductionist view, when applied appropriately, has helped us solve some of the greatest mysteries of our world.

But when reductionism is used to define the nature of human beings, it is inappropriate. It creates a misrepresentation. The answer to the question of what we "are" becomes, "just a bunch of cells." According to reductionists, human beings are **no different** than the rest of the natural world.

Another word for this is "Blobism."[3]

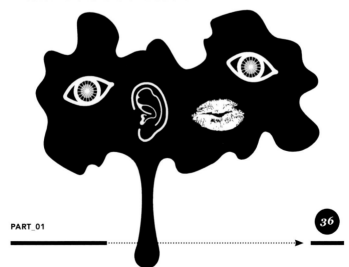

Blobism is antithetical to the Biblical description of humanity. It strips people of their worth and value. We are no longer image-bearers with a cultural mandate; rather, we are blobs left to make sense of our own reality. Stripping us of our value and worth encourages a relativistic view of morality that can, and does, lead to many human atrocities. (I recognize that religion has led to many human atrocities as well, but certain segments of our culture tend to ignore the inherent, historical danger that comes when religion is eliminated or pushed to the margins, as it was in the communist and Nazi societies of the twentieth century.) Blobs will see other people as blobs and will treat them as blobs. This makes Blobism one of the most heinous lies spreading in our world today.

The reason I started this book with the first two chapters, "Mandate" and "Talents," was to establish the worth and significance of human beings and to answer truthfully the question of what we are. I wholeheartedly reject the view of blobism. I am much more than a bunch of cells. I am God's image bearer, sharing in God's rule and administration over the earth, and I have been given a mandate to harness the natural world and develop the social world. God has given me a unique set of talents to assist my efforts in ruling the world, fulfilling the mandate, and making culture.

Culture-making doesn't happen in a vacuum. Gardens, businesses, poetry, and bridges don't just appear because God has given humans a mission, a playground, and talents. Our talents need catalysts that enable a new entity to emerge in order for culture-making (Creative Emergence) to occur.

THESE CATALYSTS ARE OUR CREATIVE HABITS.[4]

Let me illustrate. A coherent painting will not appear on a canvas if the artist has not mastered the talent of drawing shapes and mixing colors by using creative habits. A farmer will not produce crops if he has not mastered the talent of understanding soil, pesticides, and climate by using creative habits. An architect will not be able to build a bridge able to hold thousands of cars if she has not mastered mathematical equations by using creative habits.

You need another entity to grow and nurture your God-given talents so that something will emerge when you are culture-making. In other words, our talents cannot produce results unless they are aided by creative habits. This book is primarily about understanding these habits.

Creative habits by themselves accomplish nothing either, but when you combine creative habits with your talents, or creative habits with your endeavors, something will emerge.

I make no guarantees that creative emergence will always produce new and useful work. But combining creative habits with your talents and endeavors will give you the best chance for something wonderful to emerge.

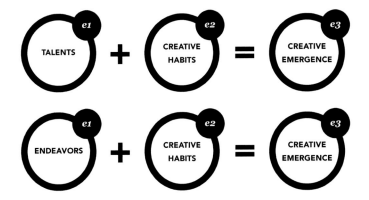

So here is the million dollar question....What happens when YOUR talents and endeavors interact with creative habits? I think this is what you hope to discover as you read this book. I believe you desire to produce culture that is good, true, and beautiful. Are you ready? Join me on a pilgrimage as we strive to fulfill the mandate God has given us. Let's combine our talents with creative habits and see what emerges. I think you will be surprised. I always am.

BUT I MUST SHARE ONE OTHER IMPORTANT FACT ABOUT THE CREATIVE LIFE BEFORE YOU LEARN HOW TO LIVE IT OUT. YOU'LL **FIND OUT** WHAT IT IS IN THE NEXT CHAPTER.

Turn the
page & see
what is hidden
INSIDE?

"RECOGNIZING WHO WE AREN'T IS ONLY THE FIRST STEP TOWARD KNOWING WHO WE ARE. ESCAPE FROM A FALSE SENSE OF LIFE-PURPOSE IS ONLY LIBERATING IF IT LEADS TO A TRUE ONE."

OS GUINNESS

THIS CHAPTER IS HIDDEN.

You will not find it in the table of contents at the beginning of the book. You will not find any numbers at the bottom of its pages. This chapter doesn't even have a name. You were unaware it existed until you got to this page or someone else told you about it.

There are many realities in life like this chapter. You are unaware they exist. One reality in particular, if left uncovered, can have a devastating effect on your life. I want to take a moment and reveal it to you.

Every semester in my creativity class, I discover that many students are pursuing talents and endeavors in light of other people's standards and expectations. They choose particular majors or nurture certain talents not because they are something they love doing, but rather because their efforts gain the attention and acceptance of their parents and peers. Some of my students are not even aware they are doing this. It is hidden from them, like this chapter. Other students know deep inside they want to follow something different but feel trapped and compelled to continue their current pursuits. It is not what they want to be or do.

The common denominator in all my conversations with such students is that their misguided pursuits are defining **who they are.** They are allowing the accolades, the applause, and the expectations of others to determine their identities. They are not becoming their true selves.

WHEN WORKING WITH INDIVIDUALS WHO ARE TRYING TO DISCOVER THEIR TRUE SELVES, **I ASK THEM TO CONSIDER A SERIES OF QUESTIONS:**

_01 Imagine you are walking in a park and you discover a statue of yourself surrounded by a beautiful landscape. What is the statue doing, holding, and wearing? There is a large plaque under the statue commemorating your life. What does it say?

_02 We often find ourselves daydreaming while we are driving or right before we take a nap. In your daydreams you might say to yourself, "If I had more time, I would…". How would you finish that statement?

_03 There are whispers, little voices in your life, that want you to take notice. We often squelch these little voices when life becomes complicated and filled with distractions. Take time this week to listen to these whispers. What are they saying?

_04 Think back to when you were a child. What activities did you enjoy? What did you do when you lost track of time?

_05 You are 90 years old and a filmmaker wants to make a documentary of your life's work. What would be the title of the film? What would the film reveal about your life's work?

_06 My favorite question, which is both the most basic and the most revealing: "What do you love doing?"

Maturity comes when you define yourself in relation to your own talents, goals, and potential rather than to somebody else's. Many people recognize they are pursuing the dreams of others but tragically continue doing it anyway. Maturity comes when we make tough choices, especially when they are different from the expectations of others. You can express your desires without being disrespectful to your parents, your loved ones, and your friends. You must articulate, with gentleness, your true passions and desires.

This is not a selfish act on your part even though it might feel that way at first. Rather, it is necessary if you are to be true to who you are and what God has created you to be. Only when you are living out your true self can you fulfill the Cultural Mandate as God intended you to.

Start by giving the above scenarios and questions considerable thought. Pursue what YOU love doing and the things that relate to YOUR talents. How do you know when you have accomplished this? A renewed passion will grow and a confidence about who you are will arise. Why? Because you will be living out your true self rather than what someone else wants you to be.

But we must take this idea of true self one step further if we are to understand how to be fully human and appropriately live out our roles on earth. Our true selves aren't limited to discovering our proper talents and pursuing our vocations. Our true selves must also be tied to our identities as "rulers" and "priests" in this world. If you recall, as image-bearers we are co-rulers with God and share in the responsibility of ruling wisely. The original plan in the garden was for us to reign with God, and it will be so in the afterlife. Just because sin has entered this world doesn't mean this responsibility has ceased. In fact, it becomes even more important.

We are God's Priests, a "holy priesthood," and we need to behave as such. We are to live a life that reflects the character of God. To rule wisely means we are to live virtuous lives so that when others gaze upon us, we become a reflection of God. That is what it means to be an image-bearer. That is what it means to be a Christian.

WHAT ARE REALLY HIDDEN IN OUR WORLD TODAY ARE IMAGE-BEARERS OF GOD; LIVES THAT REFLECT HIS GLORY AND POINT PEOPLE TO A BETTER LIFE. WE NEED TO BE FILLED WITH CHARACTER, VIRTUE, AND INTEGRITY AS WE DEVELOP OUR TALENTS AND PURSUE OUR VOCATIONS. DON'T LET THE GLORY OF GOD REMAIN HIDDEN. **LET YOUR TRUE SELF SHINE FOR THE WORLD TO SEE.**

ON COURAGE & CREATIVITY

Donald Mackinnon, in his book *In Search of Human Effectiveness*, describes courage as an essential element of creativity. The following is the kind of courage you need for creativity to flourish:

01_The courage to question what is generally accepted.

02_The courage to be destructive so that something better can be constructed.

03_The courage to think thoughts unlike anyone else's.

04_The courage to be open to experience from within and from without.

05_The courage to follow your intuition rather than your logic.

06_The courage to imagine the impossible and try to achieve it.

07_The courage to stand aside from the collectivity and be in conflict with it if necessary.

08_The courage to be and become oneself.

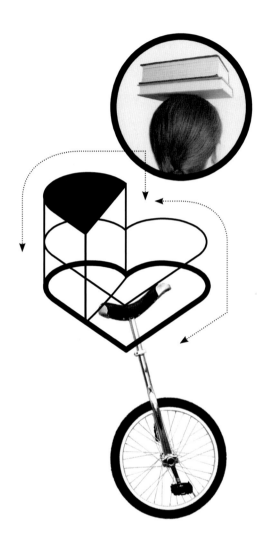

DETERMINATION

"CREATIVITY IS AN ACT OF WILL."
STEVEN PRESSFIELD

I will find any excuse not to write even though I love to write. Doesn't that seem crazy? Everything from work to entertainment to chores distracts me from writing. It's 8:46 a.m., and this morning is no different from any other. I can easily wander around the house finding excuses to stay away from my note cards or computer. Even if I make it to my computer, it takes me a lot of determination to begin typing.

How many times have you dreamed of learning an instrument, or starting a garden, or making a short film, only to be distracted by one thing: yourself? Do you find excuses not to do the very thing you want to do? I call this the Distraction of You.

Steven Pressfield gets it right when he says that "creativity is an act of the will." It is a choice we make every day. I wish it were easier, but it is not. Creativity is not a talent that some people are blessed with and others aren't. That is a myth. Creativity is a choice. It is a **way of life.**

It has been said that determination is one of the most common characteristics of Creatives.[5] The other is curiosity. Creatives throughout history have had to overcome many hardships before their creative endeavors saw the light of day. Some lacked basic resources, like money and supplies. Others lacked mentors or education. Sadly, some Creatives found themselves in communities that were hostile to their endeavors. Yet regardless of their circumstances, they took responsibility for their destinies, never placing blame at the feet of others, and were determined to keep moving forward.[6]

You need determination to live the creative life and help you overcome the Distraction of You.

In our society we want things fast. We want our food served right away and we eat it quickly (most people eat lunch in less than twenty minutes). We also want things easy. Why go to a store to get a pizza or a movie when both can be delivered to our homes? Why get off the couch to change the channel when we can use the remote?

If it's not fast and easy, we don't want it.

As I mentioned in the introduction, the creative life is anything but fast and easy. It takes determination and effort. It was Thomas Edison who said that "Genius is 1% inspiration and 99% perspiration."

When you casually observe great works of art, music, or literature, it can seem like they were created with great ease. They weren't. Successful athletes performing on the field also make it look easy. It isn't. Nor is it easy to run a successful business. Behind every great success story lies much effort and determination.

So how can you develop this type of determination? Here are a few tips to help remove the Distraction of You.

REMEMBER

You will need to constantly remind yourself why you started your endeavor in the first place. Have a note card that states the reason, the results, and the rewards of what you are doing. Read this every morning when you wake up.

GOALS

Establish short-term goals that will help you achieve your long-term goal. Focusing only on a long-term goal can be discouraging since it often seems so far away. Set several smaller goals so that you can see success as you go.

(For example, if your long-term goal is to be an artist, short-term goals could include attending a drawing class, learning how to draw a person, and visiting an art museum.)

KNOW YOURSELF

It is very difficult to develop determination if you don't know your true self. Realizing the role God has given you as an image-bearer and developing the talents you have been given are the biggest steps you can take in this area. If you still struggle to find your talents, go back to the Talents chapter and work through the series of questions listed there.

MISSION STATEMENT

Create a personal mission statement about yourself that will guide you towards accomplishing your endeavors. This statement needs to be positive, inspiring you to overcome any obstacles you will face, and it should be read aloud on a regular basis. Three to five sentences should do the trick.

(A sample mission statement for teachers: "I am an image-bearer of God who has been given the task of fulfilling the Cultural Mandate and furthering the Kingdom of God. I am a talented teacher and relationship builder, and I seek to develop these talents to their fullest potential. My mission is to educate students on the topic of history through interactive and creative experiences.")

MENTORS

Find a mentor, group, or network that can provide the appropriate amount of praise and criticism you need to accomplish your goals. I will address this at length in the Village chapter.

Are you willing to choose a creative lifestyle so that you are not the distraction keeping you from reaching your goals? Do you have the determination to push through to the end, even when things seem impossible? Are you going to take responsibility for your own destiny and rise above your circumstances, not blaming others for your situation? It takes a special person to do all this, but I know you have what it takes. You can do it. You are enough. You will always be enough.

If you are ready to roll up your sleeves and do the work needed to accomplish your dreams and goals, then you are ready to move on to Part II of this book. The next section will investigate how the combination of the two entities, creative habits and talents, will cause something to emerge and culture-making to occur.

AMABILE AND INTRINSIC MOTIVATION

What motivates you to develop a talent, start a creative endeavor, or pursue a career? Does the reward come from within or from an outside source? Teresa Amabile has discovered through her research that individuals are more motivated when the reward is intrinsic. The three facets of intrinsic motivation she found are:

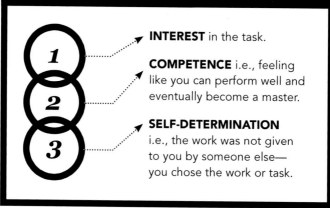

INTEREST in the task.

COMPETENCE i.e., feeling like you can perform well and eventually become a master.

SELF-DETERMINATION i.e., the work was not given to you by someone else— you chose the work or task.

PART_02

PRACTICING
CREATIVE
EMERGENCE

"CREATIVITY IS
NOT A TALENT,
IT IS A WAY OF
OPERATING."
JOHN CLEESE

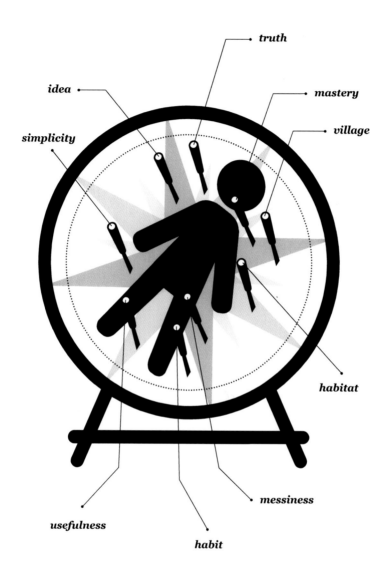

idea

truth

mastery

village

simplicity

habitat

messiness

usefulness

habit

TALENT + IDEA

"THE DIFFICULTY LIES NOT SO MUCH IN DEVELOPING NEW IDEAS AS IN ESCAPING FROM OLD ONES."
JOHN MAYNARD KEYNES

From the wheel to sliced bread to the Internet, ideas have been changing the landscape of our world for thousands of years. Without ideas there would be no pyramids, classical music, or medicinal cures. As we look to the future, ideas will continue to be humankind's means of changing the world.

What great ideas have you had lately? More importantly, where were you and what were you doing when you generated those ideas?

Have you ever had an idea pop into your mind while driving? What about when you were running or listening to a boring speaker or right before you fell asleep?

Below is a short list of what I call "idea-friendly times." Look them over and see which have helped ideas pop into your mind.

MOWING THE LAWN
LISTENING TO A SERMON
FALLING ASLEEP
EXERCISING
READING
ATTENDING A BORING MEETING
SITTING ON THE TOILET
DRIVING A CAR
TAKING A SHOWER

If you take a closer look at this list, you will discover they all have something in common. They have the potential to cause your mind to go into what is known as an 'alpha state.' When someone is in an alpha state, they are in a state of relaxation and peaceful wakefulness. They normally feel a lack of tension or anxiety, and their minds are alert to thoughts and ideas.

Thomas Edison and Salvador Dali would intentionally place their minds into an alpha state to help them generate ideas for their inventions or artwork. Edison would sit in a chair holding a heavy metal ball in each hand. As he was about to fall asleep, the metal balls would hit the floor and wake him up. He would remain seated in this relaxed state, allowing his mind to generate ideas.

Salvador Dali, similarly, would lie on his bed and hold a key in his hand. When he was about to fall asleep, the key would drop and land on a plate, waking him. He too would remain in his bed, in a tranquil state, allowing his mind to generate ideas for his art work.

You have probably experienced this many times in your life but never framed it this way. More importantly, you have likely never considered **intentionally** using idea-friendly times to help you with something called ideation—the generation of ideas.

The next time you need an idea, whether it is for a book, a business plan, a design, or a speech, try to intentionally use an idea-friendly time. For me, waking up in the morning and driving are my best times for ideation. I will intentionally lie in bed for an extra five or ten minutes to see if any new ideas pop into my mind for a project I am working on. Sometimes I get no results; other times I hit a gold mine.

Alpha states aren't the only way to generate ideas. For Creatives, ideation also occurs when they **start** a project. Rather than sitting around, hoping to be struck by lightning, they get to work. Waiting for lightning is a sure way to get discouraged and usually just leads to more sitting around. Instead, Creatives start their business plans, start their architectural designs, start their poems, start their gardens, and start playing their instruments. They recognize that ideas rarely come to us whole and complete. Only by starting and working on your endeavors will ideas begin to formulate.

MOZART ON IDEATION

"When I am, as it were, completely in myself, entirely alone, and of good cheer - say traveling in a carriage, or walking after a good meal, or during the night when I cannot sleep; it is on such occasions that my ideas flow best and most abundantly. Whence and how they come, I know not; nor can I force them..."

FAMOUS EDISON QUOTES

"I start where the last man left off."

"There is no substitute for hard work."

"I have not failed, I've just found 10,000 ways that won't work."

"Our greatest weakness lies in giving up. The most certain way to succeed is always to try just one more time."

FAMOUS SALVADOR DALI QUOTES

"Have no fear of perfection, you'll never reach it."

"Those who do not want to imitate anything, produce nothing."

"Everyone should eat hashish, but only once."

"Everything alters me, but nothing changes me."

Many of this book's ideas and concepts were born once I got started. It was doing the work of writing that allowed them to form in my mind. Action is the spark for generating ideas.

Once you get that first draft, prototype, or plan completed, you will need to let it sit for a while. Let your work marinate. This is yet another way to generate ideas. Creative people know that spending time away from their endeavor provides a new perspective when they return to it. For example, when I let my chapters marinate for a time, I find that more ideas will form in my mind, adding flavor to an otherwise dull section.

Psychologists call the process of marinating the "incubation stage." The incubation stage allows our subconscious to come up with new ideas about our project after our conscious work has been completed. What happens to us when we aren't focused on our project? Our minds are free to wander. This freedom allows ideas to come "out of the blue" when we are engaged in idea-friendly activities.

But it isn't enough to just generate ideas. We must take another step for ideation to work effectively and for something to emerge.

The other day I was eating dinner with my family when an idea popped into my head. Without saying anything, I got up, rushed to my computer, and typed the word Vampire. It would become the title of a chapter in another book I was working on, so I didn't want to forget it. Later that evening I came up with another idea for my Vampire chapter, but unfortunately I didn't write it down. It was a great idea, but I must confess that I can't remember it.

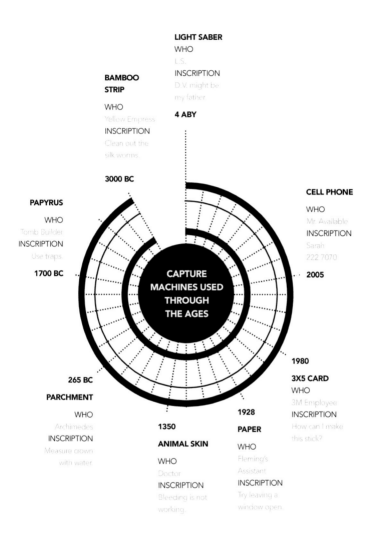

LIGHT SABER
WHO
L.S.
INSCRIPTION
D.V. might be
my father

4 ABY

BAMBOO STRIP
WHO
Yellow Empress
INSCRIPTION
Clean out the
silk worms.

3000 BC

PAPYRUS
WHO
Tomb Builder
INSCRIPTION
Use traps

1700 BC

CELL PHONE
WHO
Mr. Available
INSCRIPTION
Sarah
222 7070

2005

CAPTURE
MACHINES USED
THROUGH
THE AGES

1980

3X5 CARD
WHO
3M Employee
INSCRIPTION
How can I make
this stick?

265 BC

PARCHMENT
WHO
Archimedes
INSCRIPTION
Measure crown
with water.

1928

1350

PAPER
WHO
Fleming's
Assistant
INSCRIPTION
Try leaving a
window open.

ANIMAL SKIN
WHO
Doctor
INSCRIPTION
Bleeding is not
working.

Gold. That is what some say ideas are worth. Could you see yourself throwing a brick of gold into the ocean or throwing a $1,000 bill in a dumpster? Well, that is what I did when I failed to write down my idea. It's what we do every time we fail to capture our ideas.

Good intentions aren't enough. How many times have you had a great idea only to think, "I'll write that down when I get home"? But what happens when you get home? You forget the idea completely or remember only a fraction of it, losing the flesh and bones that made it work. Again, it's like tossing a brick of gold into the ocean.

You need a mechanism, a machine of some sort, to capture ideas the moment they are conceived. Albert Einstein and Leonardo da Vinci saw the value of this and were known for their meticulous note-taking and scribbling. Creatives make a habit of capturing all their ideas. That way they will never be forgotten . . . that is, unless you lose your idea-catching machine. (I've done that too!)

One of your first creative acts will be to build an idea-capturing machine to record ideas immediately. This could be as simple as 3 x 5 cards that you put in your car, by your bed, and on your desk. It could consist of soap chalk in the shower, or leaving yourself messages on your answering machine. Creatives use capture machines every time they come up with an idea, regardless of their location. So be sure to create a machine that is **available** and **useful** when ideas pop into your head.

NOW IT IS YOUR TURN. YOU HAVE DISCOVERED HOW TO GENERATE IDEAS BY TAKING ADVANTAGE OF IDEA-FRIENDLY TIMES. YOU HAVE ALSO SEEN THE IMPORTANCE OF CAPTURING THOSE IDEAS ONCE THEY HAVE POPPED INTO YOUR MIND. NOW TAKE SOMETHING YOU ARE CURRENTLY WORKING ON AND PRACTICE THE HABIT OF **IDEATION**. SEE WHAT EMERGES.

I SAID THIS IN THE INTRODUCTION, AND I'LL SAY IT AGAIN: I HAVE ONLY ONE RULE FOR MY STUDENTS. THE RULE IS VERY SIMPLE AND EASY TO FOLLOW. MY STUDENTS ARE NEVER ALLOWED TO SAY, "I'M NOT CREATIVE."

IT IS A LIE.

TALENT + TRUTH

"BE TRANSFORMED BY THE RENEWING OF YOUR MIND." ROMANS 12:2B

In my travels as a speaker and consultant, I am saddened by the amount of people who believe they are not creative. This false belief has prevented them from starting businesses, writing books, and finishing paintings. They neglect their callings and pursue careers and endeavors they don't really enjoy. They become shadows of their real selves, and I would argue even *less than human*, because they are not able to unleash their creative potential.

We all have voices in our heads. Some of these voices speak the truth, while others do not. No, that doesn't mean we're all crazy. These voices are what psychologists refer to as "self-talk" or "inner dialogue." Unfortunately, when our inner dialogues are distorted, they create an alternate reality, one that will keep us from seeing the world as it really is.

Having false scripts not only impacts how we perceive ourselves and the world, it influences our behavior. True scripts about our identities encourage healthy behavior while false scripts about our identities encourage unhealthy behavior.

For our purposes let's focus on the consequences of self-talk as it relates to the creative life. Check out the following scripts to the right. See if you've heard yourself say any of these things that prevent you from accomplishing your creative goals.

THESE SCRIPTS COME IN FOUR CATEGORIES:

01 / DEMANDING SCRIPTS place unrealistic expectations on our work, especially in the infancy stages of a project. "It has to be perfect" and "I must please others" are two examples of demanding scripts.

02 / BARRIER SCRIPTS belittle us and prevent us from getting started or moving forward. Barrier scripts include such sentences as "That's just not me,""I'll never be able to . . . ," and "I'm not creative".

03 / FAULTY SCRIPTS are untrue and confuse our thinking. These scripts include things like "This is the only way it can be done" and "I am not any good at . . .".

04 / EXCUSING SCRIPTS put the responsibility on someone else or something else rather than on us, where it belongs. We may find ourselves saying things like "I don't have time" and "You don't understand my situation".

Romans 12:2 says something profound about inner dialogue. It reads, "Do not be conformed to the pattern of this world, but be transformed by the renewing of your mind." Oh, how pastors distort this passage. They focus on the phrase "Do not be conformed to the patterns of this world" by listing a handful of ways to improve our behavior. This is just another form of legalism, and it is very destructive. We can never win the behavior fight.

The solution is to focus on our ***thoughts***, not on our behavior. Transformation occurs by replacing the lies we tell ourselves with the truth. By believing we are loved by God, by believing we have value and worth, by believing we are good at something, our behavior will change for the better. This is the renewing of the mind.

Carlos is a Hispanic male about six feet tall with the biggest Cheshire cat grin you've ever seen. His charisma is contagious, and you can't help but feel good after a conversation with him. He led a worship band in his youth group as a high school student and now seeks to become a worship leader at a local church.

But there used to be a dark shadow behind his great smile. Tragically, his parents and friends told him he would never be able to write music. This resulted in the following scripts: "I'm not good at writing music" and "I'll never be able to write a good song." These thoughts influenced his behavior in such a way that he never even attempted to write music. That is, until he did something about it.

One day he enthusiastically approached me after class. With that same Cheshire cat grin on his face, he said enthusiastically, "In the last eight weeks I have written 16 songs." I asked him to tell me his story and how this happened. He simply stated that he exchanged the lies his family and friends had given him for the truth. I don't know if his songs were publishable. I don't even know if they were any good. But that is not the point. He wrote music! And he loved it. He became fully human.

The creative habit of truth requires healthy scripts. It is important to discern the lies you believe and replace them with the truth. Changing your thoughts is a starting point for changing your behavior. The following are a few steps that will help you speak the truth about yourself.

STEP_01 Start listening to what you say to yourself. Record your scripts. What do you tell yourself when you want to give up? What do you tell yourself when you come to a difficult point in your project? What do you say to yourself right before you are about to show your endeavor to others or tell them about it?

STEP_02 Evaluate your inner dialogue and identify which scripts are healthy and which scripts are unhealthy (i.e. demanding, barrier, faulty, or excusing scripts).

STEP_03 Design a support plan that will help you develop healthy inner dialogue. Here are some elements that should be included in that plan:

WRITE OUT STATEMENTS ABOUT YOURSELF on a 3 x 5 card that are rational, based on facts, and true. Read the cards daily to begin the process of unlearning what is false and thinking of alternative ways to behave.

CREATE A VILLAGE (see Village chapter) that will speak the truth into your life and provide the assistance you need. Your village should provide the appropriate amount of praise and criticism to support a healthy identity.

PRACTICE THE CHRISTIAN LIFE Our focus should be on renewing the mind, and this is also accomplished by reading scripture, prayer, practicing the Sabbath, attending a local church, and participating in communion. We don't do Christian practices out of religious obligation, but rather because of how they will transform us into God's holy priesthood.

VISIT A GOOD COUNSELOR and tell him or her you would like to address possible negative scripts so you can feel better and act better.

STEP_04 Be aware of sabotage. When you start to live a healthy life, it can seem alien and foreign at first. You aren't used to it. In fact, you might even feel comfortable in your dysfunction and want to return to your former self. This is self-sabotage, and it will rear its ugly head when you are close to changing your patterns. Also, you must be aware of others who want to sabotage you. When you change, others might not like what you are becoming, so they will try to drag you back down into the pit with them. You need to hang on tightly and keep moving upwards. Sunshine waits above.

STEP_05 Begin to use your imagination. Imagine that you can do the impossible, whether you believe it or not. Imagine that you can do something well. Imagine that you can learn to master a talent.

COGNITIVE BEHAVIORAL THERAPY (CBT)

CBT is a general term for a classification of therapies which are based on the idea that our thoughts play a fundamental role in our feelings and behavior. Following this line of thought, if we change the way we think, we can feel better and act better, regardless of our situation. CBT is commonly used to treat depression, anxiety, addiction, and even phobias.

OUR THOUGHTS INFLUENCE

+ BEHA VIOR

TALENT
+ SIMPLICITY

"SIMPLICITY IS THE
ULTIMATE SOPHISTICATION."
LEONARDO DA VINCI

My brother was part-owner of a computer store in the 90's, when the profit margins for computer sales were at an all-time high. You would think he would welcome any customer that entered his store. He did not. One type of customer drove him and his employees crazy because they would waste so much time asking question after question and staying for hours and hours. This made it difficult to serve other customers who wanted to make a purchase.

He called them time-vampires. Time-vampires drained large amounts of my brother's time and energy and kept him from accomplishing what needed to be done in the store. Are time-vampires keeping you from accomplishing what you need to do?

Time and energy are limited resources. We all wish we had more of them and feel like there is never enough. Yet we allow various time-vampires to drain away this precious resource that can never be recovered.

VAMPIRES COME IN MANY DISGUISES.

Some cloak themselves as televisions. Others are camouflaged in computer screens, gadgets and gizmos, or friends who demand excessive amounts of time. If you are spending more than twenty hours a week watching television, surfing the Internet, and/or texting, you are losing the time you need to nurture and grow your talents and accomplish your endeavors. Your margins are shrinking.

Vampires can also come in the form of necessary tasks such as work, chores, and parenting.[7] If you want to complete your creative endeavors, you must set aside uninterrupted time on a regular basis to prevent life from taking over. Only effective task management will help you accomplish this.

This does not mean you must become a time management guru. Creatives manage their time in a variety of ways. Some stick to strict schedules while others don't keep a schedule at all.

What I am suggesting is task management. We simplify our lives when we reduce unimportant tasks from our weekly schedules. This will open up space to pursue our creative endeavors. To assist you with task management, use the chart on the following page to list the tasks and activities you anticipate doing this week, placing each task in one of the four categories.

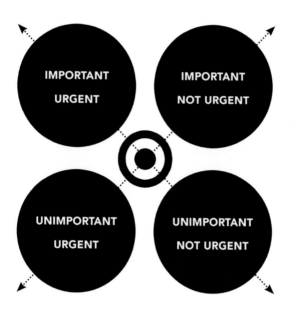

THE ACCUMULATION
OF MORE STUFF
ONLY GETS IN THE
WAY OF ACHIEVING
A SATISFYING AND
FULFILLING LIFE.

Creatives simplify their lives by not allowing unimportant tasks and activities to interfere with important and urgent tasks and activities that need their attention. This doesn't mean Creatives never watch television, or go to the beach, or have a relaxing day, but it does mean they are in control of their lives and how they will be managed.

College students always tell me they don't have any time to develop their talents and pursue their creative endeavors. I offer to bet them $1000 that I can find one to three hours per week for them to pursue their creative endeavors. No student has ever taken me up on the bet. Why? First, they know I can do it. Second, they don't want to let go of their lifestyles. They don't want to give up their unimportant tasks and activities. How sad. They are missing out on what it means to be fully human and live the creative life.

Fortunately, there are students who do make the right choices. They give up their childhood ways by making mature decisions to reduce their unimportant tasks and activities and create space to pursue their goals and dreams. Their margins widen. Their lives become simpler. They never look back.

Tasks and activities are not the only aspects of your life that must be well-managed. If you are to nurture and grow your talents, finish your endeavors, and thrive in your career, then you also need to practice the art of minimalizing. You must minimize your clutter, whether it is physical or behavioral. Everything from your possessions to your commitments to your multi-tasking must be reduced. When you reduce the clutter that is in your life, you make space for your creative self to emerge and be productive.

Embracing the simple life by practicing the art of minimizing is no easy task. In fact, committing to this kind of lifestyle can seem overwhelming. Most of us have never been taught self-moderation. It is a lost art. There don't seem to be many adults helping young people learn this very important skill. Maybe this is because so few adults practice moderation themselves.

In *The Accidental Creative*, Todd Henry believes there are three modes you can fall into while you are doing your work. They are:

DRIFTER / Someone who does whatever work they feel like from moment to moment.

DRIVER / Someone who becomes focused on outcomes but might overlook opportunities.

DEVELOPER / Someone who has a strong sense of the overall objective and approaches each task as an opportunity to develop new connections or potential ideas.

To begin living the simple life, you have to start small. Try tackling one area of your life at a time. The following is a list of suggestions for simple living. By practicing the creative habit of simplicity, you will open up space in your life to develop your talents and pursue your creative endeavors, thus allowing something to emerge.

BUY CHEAPER You don't need expensive clothes, cars, and gadgets. The more expensive an item is, the more it needs to be cared for. The more care it needs, the more time, energy, and money you will spend on it.

ELIMINATE THINGS THAT ADD STRESS TO YOUR LIFE
Make a list of your life's activities and rate each one on a stress scale from 1-10. Reduce the higher-rated activities from your life. I recognize that some things on that list are necessary, like children and work. Even so, find ways to manage them in healthy ways.

REDUCE THE UNIMPORTANT Take another look at the task chart from earlier in this chapter. If you didn't fill it out yet, do it now. Now take action and begin to reduce some of the unimportant items from your life.

PRACTICE THE #3 RULE Make a list of the things you have to do each day. Rank them. Do the top three every day. This will help you be more productive and efficient.

DON'T OVER-SCHEDULE YOUR CHILDREN We think we are good parents when we place our children in every activity available. Actually we are only teaching them to live busy lives, not better ones. Try only scheduling one or two extra-curricular activities at a time.

LEARN TO SAY NO One of the best things I learned was to say "no" to good things. By saying "no," I open the door to pursue the things I want to say "yes" to.

PURGE Reduce the clutter by getting rid of your stuff. Purge everything from clothes to gadgets.

EAT AND DRIVE SLOWLY We live such fast-paced lives, we no longer even taste our food. Enjoy some of the simple pleasures in life. This will reduce stress and anxiety.

LIVE SMALLER Buy a smaller house, a smaller yard, and a smaller car.

DO ONE TASK AT A TIME Multi-tasking is not good. Research has shown that you are more productive and more efficient when you focus on just one thing at a time.

EVALUATE NEW OPPORTUNITIES by asking, "Will this complicate my life or make it simpler?" Again, be willing to say "no" to good things.

Let me conclude with one final anecdote. I had a student, Chelsea, who made a commitment to get rid of one item a day for a year. She called it the year of simple living. One day she gave away a sweater. Another day she removed a food item from her diet completely. Her most dramatic simple act was to cut her hair so that it was easier to manage. After the year had been completed, she testified that her life had radically changed for the better because her "life became more spacious." This didn't surprise me. She practiced the creative habit of simplicity and discovered a life of freedom and joy. What about you? Why not you?

TALENT + MASTER

"PRACTICE DOES NOT MAKE PERFECT. ONLY PERFECT PRACTICE MAKES PERFECT."
VINCE LOMBARDI

"Hoping or willing something to happen won't make it happen, so get to work." This is what I tell my students who have big dreams but haven't made much effort to turn their dreams into reality. They don't like hearing this. After all, who wants to hear that it takes effort to make a dream come true? But I have to admit, I've been there before. Dreaming is so much easier.

Dreams are not bad. In fact, they are a necessary part of the creative life. They are the spark that ignites our passions and helps us see what could be. But your dreams will never see the light of day if you haven't made an effort to make those dreams come true, and the only way for your dreams to come true is to become a master of your talents and skills.

36,000,000
SECONDS

=

600,000
MINUTES

=

10,000
HOURS

=

416.666666666667
DAYS

=

1.14079614794209S
YEARS

Malcolm Gladwell, in his book *Outliers*, alludes to this when he talks about the "10,000 hours." He makes the case that if you want to be a master of a talent or skill, then you need to put in 10,000 hours of practice and experience.

Mastery comes from experience. The more we use our talents and pursue our endeavors and careers, the better we master them. At first we will feel like amateurs. We will make many mistakes and things will not turn out the way we expect. We will want to quit. Don't. Be fair to yourself, and don't expect to be perfect at the beginning of your journey. Don't compare yourself to others who have put more hours into their craft. It is self-defeating.

Mastery alone doesn't just happen through 10,000 hours of experience and practice. Creatives will tell you that **how** they practice is just as important, if not more, than how long they practice.

WHEN A CRITIC DESCRIBED HIM AS "LUCKY," SOUTH AFRICAN GOLFER **GARY PLAYER** RESPONDED WITH THESE PROFOUND WORDS, "THE HARDER YOU WORK, THE LUCKIER YOU GET."

WEISBERG THEORIES ON CREATIVITY

Weisberg set out to demystify the creative process. He believed that creativity wasn't a unique process that could only be captured by unique individuals. Rather, his research found that ideas, insights, and solutions were a result of gradual steps taken by an individual. Furthermore, he believed that creativity is enhanced by:

1_Mastery of the subject.

2_Motivation to complete a work.

3_Persistence despite failed attempts so that you can build on what you have learned. He contended that it takes 10 years of learning and practice before mastery can be achieved in a given domain.

As a former volleyball coach, I know this to be true. It was my responsibility to put the best team on the court. While lots of practice would help us achieve that goal, I knew how we were practicing would make all the difference in the world. Fortunately, I was mentored by an excellent volleyball coach at the time. Her name was Alyson, and she helped me discover this truth. Thank you, Alyson.

With her insights (brag alert!), I took a team that was 0-16 two years straight and achieved a 14-2 record in my first season. How did these girls accomplish this? We practiced. We practiced a lot. But the real secret was how we practiced. We focused on the fundamentals and practiced them over and over and over again. We joined tournaments and competed against teams who were one or two divisions higher than us. Yes, we lost every game in those tournaments, but the team was getting stronger and more proficient. We held "Wacky Wednesday" practices where every drill was designed to stretch their skills to the limit by never making an easy pass or set. Multiple distractions were added, and we attempted to replicate what would happen on the court. When it came time to play our first league game, we won.

You can use this same concept when it comes to mastering your talents. For example, if you want to be a great teacher, then you have to put in 10,000 hours of teaching experience. But you will also need to practice deliberately. Try different methods of teaching and discover how they might help you improve your craft. Find the best teachers in your area and observe them to generate new ideas for your own classroom. Read books written by the "teachers of the year" recipients. Also, have people observe your teaching who can provide appropriate levels of praise and criticism.

TALENT DEVELOPMENT

STAGE 1 / Developing an interest in a field or domain.

STAGE 2 / Honing technical skills in your field or domain.

STAGE 3 / Mastery and artistry in your field or domain.

Let's use another example. Say you want to start a business. In order to put in 10,000 hours of work and practice to master your field, find internships with successful companies in your area to get the experience and practice you need to do well. Don't ever settle for average. Rub shoulders and network with those who have experienced the ups and downs of starting businesses. Attend seminars and talk with the speakers, if you can. Offer to take the speakers out to lunch, ask good questions, and listen to what they have to say. I have done this and found the experience more educational than the conference itself.

Say you want to become a psychologist or a pastor or a social worker. Then get off your hind-quarters and get the experience and practice you need to develop your skills and talents. No one is ever ready when they take those first steps. Just go and do. Find the best schools and the best mentors, and observe the best people in your field that you can find. Record what you learn in a journal (i.e. a capture machine). In four or five years, this journal will be a treasure-trove of ideas and wisdom as you start your career or craft.

Put in the hours. Practice with a purpose. Never settle for less. Find the best.

BUT THERE IS MORE.

Miyamoto Musashi was a sixteenth century Japanese swordfighter who is known for this quote, "Never have a favorite weapon." The wisdom is simple. When you practice, don't practice the same thing over and over. Instead, tackle unfamiliar areas of knowledge and study them in depth. For example, if you want to write fiction, you also need to learn poetry and non-fiction and even biology. If you want to be a wedding photographer, you need to learn aerial photography, photojournalism, advertising photography, and even gardening. If you want to become a business manager, you also need to learn counseling techniques, developmental theories, and even architecture. Broaden and vary your knowledge and experience so that integration will occur, which will help you take your career and craft in new directions.

So how do you become a master? First, you must put in 10,000 hours of experience and practice. Second, when you practice, practice with a purpose. It means tackling other areas of knowledge and integrating what you have learned so you can take your craft in new directions.

When you have done all this, you will have become a master. From there, something will emerge.

TALENT + VILLAGE

"HOME IS NOT WHERE YOU LIVE, BUT WHERE THEY UNDERSTAND YOU."
CHRISTIAN MORGENSTERN

There is an interactive exercise I use in my class to illustrate how important it is to choose your community wisely. First, I get two volunteers and ask them to leave the classroom. Second, I place a black marker, very visible, on a table or desk. Third, I tell those students remaining in the classroom that the goal of this exercise is for the volunteers to pick up the marker. Fourth, we have each volunteer come into the room, one at a time.

When the first volunteer enters, we tell him that he needs to do a simple task. He just doesn't know what it is yet. To figure it out, he needs to start moving around listening to clues from his classmates. When the first volunteer moves closer to the marker, the students begin to shout "yeah." When he moves away from the marker, they scream "boo." The first volunteer quickly figures out what is happening and successfully picks up the marker.

The second volunteer enters the room and is given the same instructions as the first. Unfortunately, unlike the first volunteer, she begins to move around the room and only receives "boos," regardless of whether she moves closer or further away from the marker. Very soon she begins to get frustrated, which is visible in her body language. She wonders why in the world she ever volunteered in the first place. After a short while, I ask her, "How do you feel at this moment?" Her response is always similar: "I feel like giving up," "I don't know what to do," or "I'm frustrated and want to quit."

This exercise illustrates something very profound about community. If we are to achieve our goals with any level of success, then we need appropriate levels of praise (yeah) and criticism (boo). If we only hear praise, we will never receive what we need to do our careers and endeavors well. If we only hear criticism, we are likely to give up and quit.

We have all heard the sayings, "Behind every great man is a great woman" or "Behind every great woman is a great man." I don't claim to be great, but I do attribute much of my success to my adventurous, loyal, and brilliant wife, who supports my crazy undertakings. She chooses to assist me because she knows I need the help.

While my wife plays a very significant role in my life, it really takes a village for me to get my moorings and to get me pointed in the right direction. In fact, in my case it takes a rather large village to help me with my creative endeavors. What can I say? I'm needy, and I'll take all the help I can get.

My village is made up of individuals who "get it." What do people who "get it" look like? They are ones who speak the truth with gentleness and respect. They listen and remain silent when needed. They nurture my soul and tend to my dreams. They spur me on by telling me to keep moving forward. Reciprocally, they allow me to do the same for them.

Why do I congregate with others? Why do I have a village? Because I believe that living the creative life alone is unhealthy and is a recipe for failure.

The Inklings knew this to be true. They were a group of Christian writers, mostly working in fantasy and science fiction, who informally gathered together around local pubs in Oxford, England. They congregated to read aloud their works, and then to encourage, praise, and criticize them. In *Tolkien's Letters*, he called the Inkling meetings "a feast of reason and a flow of soul."

Unfortunately, usually when we study famous people in our history classes,[8] we only read about their inventions, their conquests, or their works. We rarely, if ever, hear about the village which helped them become successful. Because of this, people tend to believe that most successful people achieved their goals on their own. This is simply not true.

REGULAR MEMBERS OF THE INKLINGS

The Inklings gathered for 16 years from 1933 to 1949, producing some of the most popular works of fantasy and science fiction. Tolkien came up with the group's nickname "Inklings," referring to it as "a pleasantly ingenious pun in its way, suggesting people with vague or half-formed intimations and ideas plus those who dabble in ink."

Owen Barfield

Lord David Cecil

Neville Coghill

Victor "Hugo" Dyson

Commander James Dundas-Grant

Robert "Humphrey" Havard

Warren Hamilton Lewis

Clive Staples Lewis

Gervase Matthew

John Ronald Reuel Tolkien

Charles Williams

Behind most writers, architects, teachers, inventors, pastors, and entrepreneurs is a village that provides appropriate praise and criticism. In fact, today's Creatives continue this tradition of networking and collaborating with others because they know it is essential for success.[9]

Your village could be made up of mentors, teachers, adults, friends, or family. Choose them wisely. Just as some people know how to provide appropriate levels of praise and criticism, others will only tear you down. They become jealous and judgmental, zapping the life from you. They give bad advice and should be avoided at all costs. Proverbs 18:24 says, "One who has unreliable friends soon comes to ruin."

If you have a village that provides appropriate levels of praise and criticism, you are blessed. Put this book down right now and do something significant for them before you read on. Find a creative way to tell them you are blessed to have them. Let them know the significant role they play in your life.

Unfortunately, some of you don't have a village. Don't worry, you are not alone. There are others like you who are seeking to be part of a healthy village. Start looking for them. Keep your eye out for groups, clubs, blogs, and networks that have interests similar to your own. Join them to see if they can provide the support you need and to see if you can give them the support they need. Remember that it goes both ways.

Another option is to start your own village. Invite a few individuals in your area and see if there is any interest. Just be sure to pick individuals who can support and love you in healthy ways. Don't allow desperation to create a worse situation for you.

The following are descriptions of the types of individuals you can include in your village. You can meet with some of them in groups, while others you can meet one-on-one. Your gatherings can be formal or informal. You can meet once a week or once a month. Just find what works best for you and your village.

THE ENCOURAGERS: These wonderful people help you keep going by their kind and encouraging words. When you feel at your lowest, they are there to pick you up. They don't even have to use words; their mere presence energizes you.

THE MENTORS: These are wise individuals who have mastered their talents and careers. They have reached a point in their lives where they get joy out of training others. They take the time to teach you what is needed to develop your talents.

THE CONSULTANTS: These gifted people examine your work and provide good, sound advice. They don't seek any payment or keep a tally of things owed. They don't tell you only what you want to hear; rather, they tell you what you need to hear. They are honest and speak the truth.

THE COLLABORATORS: These are your sidekicks and your teammates on a project. They bring out the best in you, and you do the same for them. You learn to give and take from each other and trust one another's strengths. Without them, your project would be mediocre at best.

When I lived in California I was working on a screenplay with a friend of mine. She rented a space where other artists resided. It was a place where artists gathered together—where they could rub shoulders, talk about their projects, and encourage each other to move forward. What I witnessed in this "artist's village" and others like it is that when you are surrounded by other creative people, you are more likely to be creative and productive yourself. Rock stars hang out with rock stars.

Joining a village is not optional. You need it to be healthy, you need it to be productive, and you need it to be creative. Join or start one today.

TALENT + HABITAT

"THE IMPORTANT THING, HOWEVER, IS TO HAVE A SPECIAL SPACE TAILOR-MADE TO ONE'S OWN NEEDS, WHERE ONE FEELS COMFORTABLE AND IN CONTROL." MIHALY CSIKSZENTMIHALYI

Your surroundings affect the way you think and create whether you want them to or not. From colors to scents to music to lighting, everything shapes the way your brain thinks.

DON'T BELIEVE ME?

A study was done by the University of British Columbia in which researchers analyzed the effect of color on students' cognitive abilities. A sample of 666 students (a number I would not have chosen, but a good sample size nonetheless) between the ages of 17 and 39 years old were asked to solve various problems on a computer screen. Each screen had either a red, blue, or white background. What they discovered was amazing.

The students scored higher on detail-oriented assignments when they used screens with red backgrounds, while the group using blue backgrounds did better on tasks requiring imagination. In other words, we take cues from hues.

But the researchers didn't stop there. They also wanted to see how sound affected creativity. They assigned 65 college students to take a test called the Remote Associate Task (RAT) and placed them under four different sound conditions: low-noise, moderate-noise, high-noise, and no-noise. What they discovered was that moderate levels of noise can cause a distraction, which can lead to higher levels of creativity. However, too much noise can create too much of a distraction, which hinders the brain from processing, and thus leads to lower levels of creative output.

What researchers are discovering is that our spaces, or habitats, can play a significant role in the types of output our brains produce. Colors, sounds, lights—any components of atmosphere—influence productivity.

Consider this. If you were to visit a historic downtown Chicago loft building in Haymarket Square, you would find one of the most creative meeting and event spaces in the country. Developed by Eva Niewiadomski, Catalyst Ranch[10] provides a variety of colorful spaces which can, as she says, "add spice and creativity to a group's meeting." Businesses and Creatives are willing to spend money to use her spaces to help infuse creativity into their work. Why? They believe habitats make a difference and are willing to spend money based on that belief.

What does your space look like? How much creativity is infused into your environment? Is your space made up of four white walls with a few pictures? That won't cut it. Are you in a small cubical with blue or gray fabric? That's a recipe for getting fat, not creative.

It's time to change your space. You don't need to spend a lot of money to make your space fit your needs. In fact, try to avoid designing it like a show room or a prop for others to gawk at. You might be able to impress others with your decorations, but it doesn't help you do your work. Instead, design it to help you be productive.

At my school I got permission to paint three colors on my walls. I even painted a small, orange square on one wall as a reminder to think outside the box, to think in the box, to think about multiple boxes, and to think that there is no box. I brought in a bold red couch and some bean bags to help induce idea-friendly times. My home office has many of the same features. The difference is my walls at home are lined with European board games I have collected over the past decade. I also light a scented candle as a ritual to start my work, and I warm up a comfort cob (corn wrapped in fabric

We Take Cues From Hues

filled with cinnamon) to place on my knees while I write. The smell and warmth from the comfort cob seems to do the trick. I have no rationale for it, but it works for me.

What kind of environment do you need? Would it help to have various symbols or icons or sayings on your wall for daily inspiration? Are you more on the wild side and in need of loud noises, vivid colors, and hanging bicycles to inspire your thoughts? Or do you require a simple space with bright colors and comfortable chairs? In my experience, and from what I hear from other Creatives, there is no specific recipe for creating the best habitat. It is all about creating a habitat that works for you.

Some critics do not believe environments really influence creativity. They contend that there is no real evidence for it. They have a right to that position. But look around at other successful Creatives and see what they do with their spaces. It's clear they believe their environments affect them.

PIXAR'S EMERYVILLE HEADQUARTERS

As Pixar's CEO, Steve Jobs wanted to design an office building that would encourage unplanned collaboration among the computer scientists, animators, writers, accountants, and everyone in between. So he dreamed up a large atrium where all the employees' mailboxes would be housed, the only campus restrooms existed, and the cafeteria, fitness center, and large theater were located. Brad Bird, who directed *The Incredibles*, said of this space, "The atrium initially might seem like a waste of space...But Steve realized that when people run into each other, when they make eye contact, things happen."

I believe this myself. That is why I practice the creative habit of habitat. I infuse my environment with anything that invigorates, motivates, and inspires my creativity. Below are a few suggestions for inspiration:

WHITEBOARDS: Get several of them. Line your walls with them. Write your goals on them. Write your core values on them. Write problems you want to solve, possible solutions, an outline of the book you want to write, etc. As an alternative, draw pictures to illustrate your thoughts rather than using words. Creative people do this all the time. Try it.

PAINT: Use colors that help you feel safe, comfortable, energetic, loud, or all these things together. Paint a mural on one of your walls. Hang some of your own paintings. You could even paint words that represent your core values, such as Attitude, Simplicity, Balance, Health, and Fun.

COUCH: Lie down and listen to music. This will allow your brain to relax and let new ideas flow. Naps are good, too.

WALL DRESSING: Hang stuff on your walls. I have seen bicycles, snowshoes, t-shirts, and clocks covering wall space. Movie posters, book posters, and inspirational posters are used as wallpaper. Which reminds me, you can use wallpaper as well.

CANDLES: A burning candle provides an excellent way to calm your mind and entice your sense of smell. I light a candle as a cue to tell me it is time to write.

FUN STUFF: Include fun stuff like lava lamps, gadgets, Dr. Seuss books, Play-Doh, Legos. Such items will bring out the child in you, which is essential for your imagination.

TALENT
+ MESSINESS

"IF WE ARE NOT WILLING TO FAIL, WE CANNOT DO ANYTHING ORIGINAL."
SIR KEN ROBINSON

We live in a win-lose culture: winners on one side and losers on the other. If you want to amount to something, you'd better be on the winning side. Just watch parents who go berserk at Little League baseball games. Between yelling at umpires and impossible expectations for their kids, they teach their children that winning is everything.

From birth we are told to win.[11] We have to win at grades, sports, and Monopoly. If we don't, then we lose . . . and losing is bad. So we fear failure.

The fear of failure paralyzes us. It keeps us from taking those first few steps, from experimenting with ideas, or from finishing our creative endeavors. After all, how will people view us if we fail? Don't we need to succeed in order to be loved, accepted, and significant?

There is good news! Our worth and significance cannot be found in our performance. Instead, they have already been determined through Christ's actions rather than our own. When we try to measure up to other people's standards and fail, we bring about anxiety and depression. Have you experienced this?

Before I became a recovering striver, I sought love and acceptance through my behavior and performance. I use the word recovering because sometimes I go back to my old patterns and have to remind myself that Christ's performance, not mine, determines my worth.

What we need to realize is that all Creatives have rough starts and encounter many failures along the way. We tend to focus on the successful parts of Creatives' endeavors—in other words, the final product. We haven't taken the time to examine the process Creatives went through to achieve their goals. I believe this is tragic, since understanding the process is the key to success.

If you want to find deliverance from the fear of failure, you need to change your perspective. Creative people view failure as success. Rather than seeing the world as win-lose, they see it as win-learn. I have made many mistakes in my life, and I have learned from each one. They helped me get where I am today. After all, how many failures—or I should say, lessons learned—did Thomas Edison experience before he saw the light? 2,200. How many times did the following authors get

ANNE LAMONT is known for providing instructions on the writing life in her book *Bird by Bird*. If you want good advice on how to get started, writing a terrific third draft, and overcoming perfectionism, read chapters 2-4. The book you are holding in your hands went through a Chapter 3 draft. During that process, I did not feel enthusiastic or confident. I had to push through and keep moving forward, despite what I felt and what I was producing.

Tolstoy rewrote War & Peace eight times. This was before typewriters and computers.

rejected by publishers and agents before finding a publisher? John Grisham: 26; Frank Herbert: 23; Stephen King: 30; J.K. Rowling: 12; Dr. Seuss: 27. How many last-second shots did the greatest basketball player ever, Michael Jordan, miss? He is known for this statement, "I've missed more than 9000 shots in my career. I've lost almost 300 games. 26 times, I've been trusted to take the game winning shot and missed. I've failed over and over and over in my life. And that is why I succeed."

As I mentioned before, I used to coach volleyball. Remember how I bragged about how well my team did? Well, let me tell you about a big blunder I made one season. We were playing a team that had gone undefeated for the past two years. The girls and I had prepared for the game and were ready to bring these Goliaths down. We were in the last set of the game, winning 12 to 7, when the other team called for a timeout. They knew they were in trouble since we were only 3 points away from winning. When the girls formed a huddle around me, I said with confidence, "You girls are doing great. We have them right where we want them. They are scared and unable to focus. Go out there and finish this game." Guess what? The other team came out and proceeded to score 8 straight points.

It wasn't the girls' fault they lost that day. It was completely and totally mine. I failed them as a coach. What I should have said to them in that huddle was, "Don't think for a minute this game is over. The other team is going to come out and play harder than they have played all day. They are not about to lie down and quit. Keep your focus."

I have logged this event in my failure resume. Unlike a standard resume where you list your jobs, accomplishments, education, and awards, this is where I list my failures. I have many speaking, coaching, and ministry faux pas. The point isn't to get others to feel sorry for me or wallow in my misery, but rather to record what I have learned from these experiences. This resumé changes my perspective from win-lose to win-learn. This slight change of perspective is significant enough to keep me moving forward. Now if I ever find myself in a similar coaching situation, I'll know what to do.

Another failure of mine was my first attempt at writing a screenplay titled *The Last Guardsman*. It's a fish-out-of-water story where a barbarian is mistaken for a Republican Guardsman and brought back to the Capitol. Unfortunately, the dialogue and story structure were horrible. Fortunately, I didn't see this endeavor as a failure. First, I celebrated the accomplishment of writing a 120-page script. (After all, I badly needed the practice as I was learning how to write screenplays.) Second, I realized I had to roll up my sleeves and commit to seriously learning the concepts of story structure and dialogue. As I started, I took a few classes at a local film school. After whetting my appetite and feeling a bit more confident, I started a Master of Fine Arts program in creative writing to learn even more. The hours I have put in have paid off, as I am writing better stories and have the opportunity to teach story structure in a Comics and Sequential Art class at the University. I am glad to say that my second script is much better than the first. However, *The Last Guardsman* taught me a lot about writing and what I needed to do to become a better writer. I will always treasure that script.

The creative life is filled with failures and mistakes. If you are not willing to fail, you will not be able to create anything new or original. More importantly, if you see a ***single failure*** as a ***total failure***, you will never be able to develop your talents, finish your endeavors, and/or grow in your career. I have witnessed this firsthand with students who have given up completely because of just one failed attempt. It is tragic.

THE DOT

What makes a great children's book is that it also has something profound to say to adults. Written by Peter H. Reynolds, **The Dot** is no exception to the rule. It is about a girl named Vashti who stubbornly believes she is not creative. But her teacher knows differently and helps her on a journey of self-discovery.

HER TEACHER SMILED. "JUST MAKE A MARK AND SEE WHERE IT TAKES YOU."

One way Creatives overcome their fear of failure is by developing a willingness to start out messy. Creatives recognize that **all** creative endeavors must start out messy if they are going to eventually become useful. It is unavoidable. Whether it is your first sketch, first draft, or first business proposal, messy is the recipe for success. Sure you will need to make changes, adjustments, and maybe even an overhaul, but first you need to make a mess to get where you want to go.

Imagine building a deck. Tools are laid out, wood is scattered all over the lawn, and beams are sticking up out of the ground. It's so far from how you imagined it to be. Yet it must go through this messy process before it can be completed.

While perfectionism can be a great asset in the latter part of an endeavor, it is most certainly a liability in the beginning stages of creativity. Our false belief that we need to have it "just right" the first time prevents us from completing our task and realizing our dreams.

For example, as I write this page I am getting my thoughts down without worrying about grammar, flow of thought, or even if what I'm writing is publishable. Right now it is an English teacher's nightmare and doesn't make any sense. It needs an overhaul.

I have to admit that it took a long time for me to be able to write this way. I wanted my writing to be readable on my first draft. And if it wasn't, I would give up. Many of my early creative endeavors were never completed because I wanted them to be right the first time; I wanted them to be perfect.

Creative people, even ones who are perfectionists, realize the importance of practicing the creative habit of messiness. They know that if they want to create something original, they must be willing to be messy and fail often. It is essential for making something beautiful. Remember, you are the only person who has to see this first draft.

A FINAL THOUGHT: MOST CREATIVE ENDEAVORS ARE NEVER FULLY COMPLETE. TAKE THIS BOOK, FOR EXAMPLE. IT COULD STILL BE IMPROVED UPON. IT'S NOT PERFECT, IT IS A BIT MESSY IN SOME PLACES, AND A FEW PORTIONS COULD BE EXPANDED. BUT AT SOME POINT I HAD TO LET IT GO. I HAD TO RELEASE THIS PROJECT. OTHERWISE, IT WOULD HAVE NEVER BEEN PUBLISHED AND NOTHING WOULD HAVE EMERGED.

"IF YOU WANT TO
CHANGE A HABIT,
YOU MUST FIND AN
ALTERNATIVE ROUTINE,
AND YOUR ODDS
OF SUCCESS GO UP
DRAMATICALLY WHEN YOU
COMMIT TO CHANGING
AS PART OF A GROUP.
BELIEF IS ESSENTIAL,
AND IT GROWS OUT OF A
COMMUNAL EXPERIENCE,
EVEN IF THAT COMMUNITY
IS ONLY AS LARGE AS TWO
PEOPLE."

CHARLES DUHIGG

TALENT
+ HABIT

Most people who start a creative endeavor quit. They begin with grandiose dreams and hit the ground running. The first few days or weeks seem like magic. Then they hit a wall. The enthusiasm that was there in the beginning fades away like a wilting flower and is not enough to get them through the tough times.

Have you experienced this before? You start out just fine only to give up after a day, a week, or a month. Like you, I have experienced this on several occasions. I lacked the desire needed to get over the tough times and rough spots. This occurs when we believe that our dreams and goals *are the same as habits*. They are not.

Once again we'll take a lesson from other Creatives. What do they use to assist themselves to keep moving forward with their endeavors? What's their secret?

They make a habit of making habits.

Enthusiasm, dreams, and novelty will only motivate us in the short run. What we need are habits that keep us moving forward when we lose that feeling of grandeur. What we need is something to activate us when we want to quit.

Old habits are hard to break and new habits are difficult to form. Fortunately, the latest research in neuroscience tells us that when good behaviors are repeated over and over again, our brains will imprint these patterns to cut down energy use, thus freeing up our minds to perform other important actions. At the same time, our brains are creating new electronic pathways that make it easier to perform these actions every time we repeat them.

The implications are simple. In order to form a new habit, you have to perform an action repeatedly to imprint it onto the brain. Eventually these actions will become automatic.

In my M.F.A. program, I had to write a screenplay in eight days. A screenplay normally consists of ninety to one hundred twenty pages. Do the math. I had to write twelve to fifteen pages a day. At that rate, I did not have a chance to look back and do much rewriting, if any. By the time I was on page sixty-five, my protagonist had changed and my first act did not coincide with my third act. But onward I went. Finally, I hit one hundred seven pages. It was the world's worst screenplay.

But even though it was a terrible script, I had finished. I did what few people had done: I completed a screenplay from beginning to end. We were to take day nine off and reward ourselves for the great accomplishment we had just achieved. As a collector of European style board games, I went out and bought a game.

On day ten we were back at it again and had to rewrite our script in only six days. My script went from "the world's worst" to "the world's second worst." Once it was completed, we were to reward ourselves again. This process was repeated over and over. It helped us form behaviors that would become automatic. We were developing a writer's life.

The following are a few things I learned regarding habit formation. Each step has allowed me to develop my talents and complete several creative endeavors, like this book you are reading.

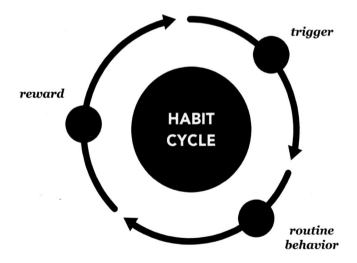

_01 / CREATE TRIGGERS

Behavior formation needs something to help it get started. It needs what psychologists call a "trigger." Triggers alert us to actions that must be performed. In order for triggers to be effective, they must cause us to stop what we are doing and force our brains to consider a new course of action. Also, the same trigger must be used over and over again. When your trigger occurs, you must perform your task immediately. You cannot put it off. Below are some examples of triggers other Creatives have used to assist them with various tasks.

TASK / Practice Music

TRIGGER / Hang a sign across the doorway to your bedroom door so you have to remove it to enter. Then begin practicing.

TASK / Running

TRIGGER / Put running shoes and clothes by your bed so you step on them when you wake up.

TASK / Homework

TRIGGER / Have a friend call you.

TASK / Writing

TRIGGER / Place a candle on the middle of your desk. Light the candle as a reminder to focus on your writing and not get distracted.

_02 / CREATE REWARDS

While many rewards occur intrinsically as a result of doing your tasks, like learning a language, or completing a business plan, or losing weight, you can implement other additional rewards to motivate you to form good habits. Rewards can occur weekly, monthly, or at the end of an endeavor.

Rewards can vary, depending on the person. Here are a few treats Creatives have rewarded themselves with: a dinner date to a nice restaurant, a gift, a vacation, a specialty coffee drink, a movie, or a trip into the city.

_03 / VISUALIZE

To provide additional support for our triggers and rewards, we need to begin visualizing ourselves performing the habit. Visualization entails watching yourself doing the habit and receiving the benefits of accomplishing your goal. But don't just imagine it all going smoothly—it's also important to imagine the obstacles you will face, and watch yourself overcoming them in healthy ways. A good time for visualization is when you wake up in the morning. Remain in bed for an additional five minutes and imagine yourself carrying out the habit that you want to accomplish that day.

_04 / ADD A VILLAGE MEMBER

Never try to develop a new habit on your own. We are made to live in community. Bring someone (or several people) into this process. Add a member to your village (review the Village chapter) who is smart, tender, and affirming, and who will keep you accountable to the routine you are developing.

Accountability is largely misunderstood in our culture today. We tend to believe accountability happens when we report our actions, whether they're successful or not, to someone we respect. This is simply not true. Accountability is much more than giving a progress report. In this false version of accountability, what happens when you fall short of your goal? Often you get a pat on the shoulder or a little reprimand. That is not enough. That is not accountability.

The person who is holding you accountable must have power or authority over you. Sound scary? It is if that person isn't safe. But with the right person(s), those who are tender yet consistent, it can be life-forming.

The person who holds you accountable must be able to apply consequences to your actions. You learn responsibility when consequences are part of the program. I am not suggesting authoritative accountability in which consequences undermine your desire to flourish. You should have a discussion with your village members to determine appropriate consequences. Talk over what would best motivate you. But remember, in order for consequences to be effective, they must sting a little bit.

_05 / REPETITION

Some say it takes twenty-one days to start a habit. Others argue it takes thirty. Some even suggest longer. It might be different for different people—I don't really know. But what I do know is that the routine must be repeated over a long period of time if a behavior is to become automatic. It takes time. Don't stop. Keep moving forward.

_06 / BELIEVE

None of my earlier suggestions regarding habit formation
will help unless you decide to change your old habits. It is an
act of the will, and only you can make the choice to change.
You must believe the habit you are forming is good, you
must believe the habit you are forming is right, and you must
believe the habit you are forming is in your best interest. If you
don't have that confidence, the whole foundation will crack
and your new habit will collapse after a small tremor.

_07 / RENEW THE MIND

Let us not forget that what we think about ourselves influences
our feelings and actions. We must replace false scripts with
true ones if we desire to exercise healthy behaviors.

Once your mind has been renewed and you believe in what
you are doing, you can apply triggers, rewards, visualization,
a village, and repetition to help you form your habits. Try
practicing the creative rhythm of habits and see what emerges.

TALENT +
USEFULNESS

"BY PREVAILING OVER ALL OBSTACLES AND DISTRACTIONS, ONE MAY UNFAILINGLY ARRIVE AT HIS CHOSEN GOAL OR DESTINATION." CHRISTOPHER COLUMBUS

It would be a bold move to label someone spiritually useless. But two thousand years ago, in a letter composed by the risen Christ to the church in Laodicea, that is exactly what happened. The letter describes the Laodiceans' spiritual condition, using water as a metaphor (see Revelation 3:14–22).

To understand this metaphor, one must understand the letter's historical and cultural context. Outside the city of Laodicea, there were two sources of water—a cold stream and a hot spring. The hot water was useful for cleaning clothes and dishes, while the cold water was pleasant to drink. But problems occurred when residents returned to the city with the water they'd gathered. By then it had become lukewarm. It was *useless*. This is how Jesus described the spiritual condition of the Laodicean Christians—spiritually useless.

The Laodiceans became spiritually useless because they no longer trusted God for their well-being. Rather, the gold, clothes, and medicine they had developed and acquired allowed them to believe they had everything they needed. As a result, they could no longer be effective witnesses to other Laodiceans who were following pagan gods. God called these Christians "wretched, pitiful, poor, blind, and naked."

This letter to the Laodiceans is still relevant today. We too can become spiritually useless. While the Laodiceans had gold, clothes, and medicine to keep their eyes from focusing on God, today, we have other distractions that produce the same effect. In my recent years of teaching and coaching, I've discovered three common distractions that keep people from becoming spiritually useful. Let's take a look to see if you have been lured by any of them.

TECHNOLOGY

I could write an entire book on this topic. But at this point I've chosen an easier way to teach people about it: I do seminars titled, "Escaping the Wet Life." The wet life is the real world we live in, made up of flesh and blood. The virtual world, on the other hand, is made up of silicon, metal, and electricity. Let's take a look at two phenomena that have occurred over the past decade since the creation of the virtual world.

The first phenomenon is one in which individuals **prefer** to be in the virtual world over the real world. They desire to escape the wet life. Imagine you are an average person, by the world's standards, in appearance, intelligence, and social graces. Turn on the computer, and soon you can create your own reality, one in which you are at the top of the totem pole. For example, you can become a level thirty warrior leading sixty individuals on a dragon raid, or you can create Facebook and Pinterest sites that make you look hip and cool, or you can design avatars that outshine any supermodel. As a result, people spend twenty to sixty hours per week online living their alternate lives. They no longer desire to live in the real world. In their attempts to escape the wet life, they no longer want to develop their talents for culture-making. They just want to be in their rooms with their computers. They have become spiritually useless.

The second phenomenon occurs whenever we check a Tweet, or achieve a level in a game, or discover a funny video online. Each time these things happen, a neurotransmitter called dopamine is activated in our brains. Dopamine passes electronic messages, the type of messages that make us want things, especially things that are new and pleasurable. In other words, dopamine is essential for humans if they are to have any desire to seek things that are new and useful. Since we are already satisfying our need to discover new things every time we answer our Tweets, achieve a level in a game, or discover a funny video, we are ***losing our desire*** to create new things in the real world. We still might care about the many social problems in our world, but we don't do much about them. We have become spiritually useless.

Before I go any further I should point out that I am not telling you to throw away all your technology. But for some of you, going "cold turkey" might be a healthy choice. I have a computer, and I do enjoy an occasional video game. But I must be careful that I don't fall prey to the lure of technology and become a dopamine addict.[13] Otherwise, I too, would become spiritually useless.

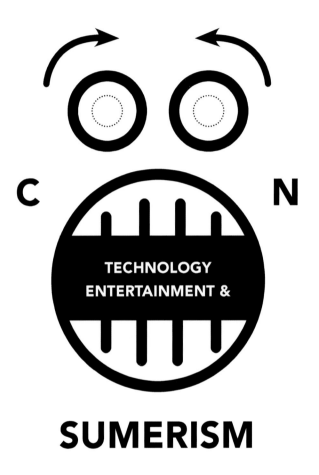

C N

TECHNOLOGY
ENTERTAINMENT &

SUMERISM

ENTERTAINMENT

What do you live for? In the past, people desired to grow crops, or start businesses, or educate children. Now that is no longer the case. Instead, I see people living for entertainment. They see their hobbies, books, and screen time more as a **_vocation_** than a pastime. This is becoming normal and seen as appropriate and good. Is it true for you?

The allure of entertainment has **_replaced_** our desire to be productive. Think about where you put most of your mental energy. Do you dream of making lots of money so you can retire early? Is free time beginning to take over a large portion of your week? When you schedule your time, is your focus on how you can best maximize entertainment time, or how you can best be a productive individual?

We are in the middle of an interesting cultural paradox. Right now many people are becoming workaholics, while at the same time, others are becoming Playaholics.

Playaholics are spiritually useless because they worship created things rather than the Creator (Romans 1:21-25). For them the cultural mandate has been turned upside down. By serving created things rather than serving the Creator and fulfilling the cultural mandate, they have lost sight of what truly matters in this world and what it means to be a follower of Christ. They are content to fill their own appetites with entertainment.

CONSUMERISM

What is the ideal lifestyle? This is not an easy question to answer. The National Survey of Youth and Religion[14] reveals that the majority of emerging adults (ages 18-23) see the ideal life as being financially secure and having material comfort. At first, this might seem like a fairly decent answer. Unfortunately, the Laodiceans would have answered the same way.

The consumerist mentality has always been around, especially in capitalist societies. However, it seems like it is becoming even more prevalent today. Some propose this is because parents give their children whatever they want (as opposed to what they need), especially when they pout, cry, or scream. Others claim our culture promotes the belief that the amassing of wealth is a good thing, something to aspire to. While these things do, to some degree, socially determine our thoughts, and therefore shape our habits, I believe the problem goes much deeper.

We consume because we are unhappy, empty, bored, and dissatisfied. Furthermore, we are depressed, anxious, and dysfunctional. The media and advertisers know this and spend millions of dollars telling us that consuming their products will satisfy our hunger. Unfortunately, we buy (pun intended) into this lie with open arms.

The only cure for all of this is to do our work. We have to put down the Cheetos, turn off the computer, get off our hind-quarters, simplify our lives, and act.

So what is the ideal lifestyle? I would like to recommend a better alternative to consumerism. This would entail: 1) Rising above the acquisition of material belongings; 2) Discovering your talents and using them for culture-making; 3) Realizing your true self and becoming fully human; 4) Preferring to live in the real world over the virtual world; 5) Avoiding a life of immorality; 6) Being a loving, kind, and gentle person; 7) Having the courage to stand up for what is right; 8) Becoming a mature adult; 9) Treating others with respect; 10) Being spiritually useful.

So, have you fallen under the spell of technology, entertainment, and/or consumerism? If you have, you are not alone. I have been there too. Fortunately, there is good news. Now that you are aware of your circumstances, you can make a critical decision to change. This is a pivotal moment. Which choice will you make?

"Social determinism"[15] is the belief that social interactions and exchanges alone determine behavior. According to this theory, our consumerist society determines how we see and view our world. It shapes our minds and determines our choices and actions. But I don't believe social determinism alone determines our behavior. We have free will. In fact, our free will allows us to rise above the noise and confusion of our culture. It is your will that can help you choose to become spiritually useful.

The risen Christ states, in the same letter to the Laodiceans, "I stand at the door and knock. If anyone hears my voice and opens the door, I will come in and eat with them, and they with me." This was not written to non-believers, as some preachers have misquoted for evangelistic purposes. The Laodicians were believers, and this verse is a call for Christ-followers who have become spiritually useless to change their ways.

Fortunately, we have a loving God who pursues us. It is only by his action—his Son's shed blood—that we are redeemed. It is never by our own efforts. What is truly amazing is that God wants to use us—broken and sinful people that we are—to bring peace and restoration to the earth. Discovering our role in God's story of redemption can provide a sense of meaning and purpose for our lives and helps us prioritize what is important.

The fall (see Genesis 3) has had a devastating impact on our world. Just grab a newspaper or turn on the news and you'll see a world filled with war, famine, suffering, disease, heartache, and pain.

If we want to become spiritually useful, we need to be good stewards of the talents God has given each of us and use them to move humanity closer to the Almighty. Our work doesn't have to be well-known or change governments or reach millions of people for it to be useful and redemptive. I believe there are books out there that have never been published and have only been read by a handful of people that may be the most-redemptive literature ever written. There are Creatives who are changing the lives of a few people in dramatic ways through their careers, but we will never know or hear of their courageous acts. There are individuals who have embraced values and purposes that transcend the accumulation of wealth, at much sacrifice, but their stories will not be told to the masses.

Our western society measures success very differently than God does. Our society believes we all must strive to be the biggest and the best. Don't get caught up in this way of thinking.

We have only one audience. He is the Alpha and Omega. We do our work for Him. As I write this book, I have no idea how the world will receive it. Sure, I would love to sell thousands of copies, but while it may reach only a few readers, this work is really for the One to whom I'm accountable at the end of the day. I hope I have followed God's mandate, used creative habits to help me along the way, and produced a work that is useful.

THE RISEN CHRIST ENDS HIS LETTER WITH THESE CLOSING REMARKS, "TO THOSE WHO ARE VICTORIOUS, I WILL GIVE YOU THE RIGHT TO SIT WITH ME ON MY THRONE, JUST AS I WAS VICTORIOUS AND SAT DOWN WITH MY FATHER ON HIS THRONE. WHOEVER HAS EARS, LET THEM HEAR WHAT THE SPIRIT SAYS TO THE CHURCHES."

PART_03

ADDITIONS

"I NEVER
WORRY ABOUT
ACTION,
BUT ONLY
INACTION."
WINSTON
CHURCHILL

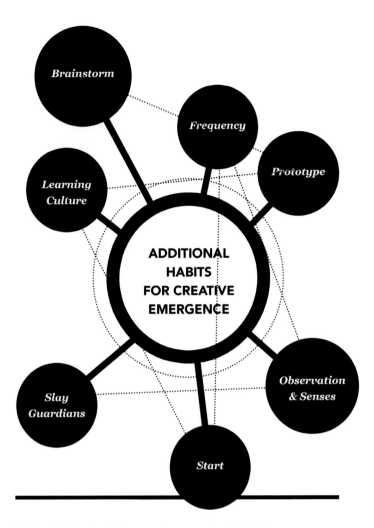

Brainstorm

Frequency

Prototype

Learning Culture

ADDITIONAL HABITS FOR CREATIVE EMERGENCE

Observation & Senses

Slay Guardians

Start

While this book addresses nine creative habits in detail, there are many more that can be practiced to unleash your creative potential. Try each one and see what emerges as a result.

FREQUENCY / Try changing your routine for a day. Change the order of your morning ritual of showering, eating, and brushing your teeth. Choose a different route to work. Sit on the other side of your desk. Sit in a different chair. Practice this once a month to give your brain a jolt. New perspectives and ideas might emerge.

PROTOTYPE / See what emerges when you design several prototypes of your idea. For example, write five different poems on the same subject, or draw out four separate designs for a room, or create three different business proposals. Look them over and then combine the best elements from each one.

BRAINSTORM / See what emerges when you use thinking tools for ideation. *Thinkertoys*, by Michael Michalko, is a book filled with idea-generating tools to help you come up with the right idea. Try some of them out and see what emerges.

LEARNING CULTURE / See what emerges when you begin to learn subjects outside your talents, endeavors, and career. Leonardo da Vinci saw the importance of systematic thinking and sought to learn from both art and science. When you combine other subjects with your endeavors, you will be able to take them into new directions.

OBSERVATION + SENSES / See what emerges when you observe the world using all of your senses. Don't just read about trees; in addition, try smelling, tasting, touching, seeing, and listening to them. You will learn so much more about the subject you are studying and heighten your observation skills.

START / Just start. Beat procrastination and perfectionism by taking that small step.

SLAY GUARDIANS / See what emerges when you name and label all the obstacles that are in your way. These obstacles, or guardians, exist both inside and outside our lives. With help from your village, formulate a plan to overcome them, and see what emerges.

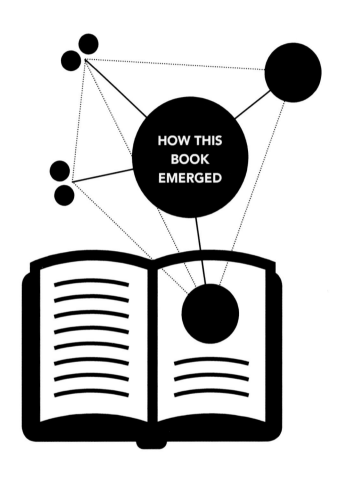

HOW THIS
BOOK
EMERGED

The following pages provide a snapshot of how this book emerged, using the creative habits I have described. I don't claim to have my act together, so please don't misinterpret what I am attempting to do here. I struggle. I doubt. I get distracted. Since this is very true in my life, I see the need to practice creative habits. They are essential to my ability to complete projects. I hope the following will further illustrate how to practice creative emergence.

IDEATION / My most idea-friendly times for this project were while I was driving, waking up in the morning, and just sitting on a couch. About three times a week I intentionally attempted to go into an alpha state, and if an idea emerged, I captured it on a 3x5 card.

TRUTH / My inner dialogue vacillated from true scripts to false ones. At times I thought my work wasn't very good, and I wondered why I was writing this book. Other times I thought I had something new and useful to say and plunged forward. As a Professor of Creativity, I felt pressure to create the most creative book ever. The expectations were downright impossible to meet. I had to speak the truth to myself and not attempt to meet those expectations. I had to write what was on my heart and in my mind and hope it would make a difference.

SIMPLICITY / It is normal for me to have several projects going on at the same time. I have a screenplay that needs to be converted into a novel, I'm working on a children's book concept based on a true story, and I'm trying to finish designing a couple of board games. I had to set those projects aside to focus on this particular task. This was not easy for me. I like to juggle lots of things at once.

MASTER / It took me several years of study, the teaching of a creativity class over forty times, and the completion of an M.F.A. in creative writing, to get to where I could write a book about creativity. But I still felt like an amateur compared to others in the same field. That said, I continued to put in the hours I needed to master this subject well.

VILLAGE / Go to my acknowledgements to discover my village. I am blessed.

HABITAT / I sat in my office down in my basement, surrounded by a hundred European board games. I had two desks. One table was used for scribbling on note cards and mapping out the book, the other table was for typing on the computer. I put a heated comfort cob on my legs and placed my hands on it to keep them warm while I was thinking (I live in Michigan, but I'm originally from California and get cold). At times I went to various coffee shops to change my perspective and surroundings.

MESSINESS / The first draft was really a mess. I did not start out with a linear model, knowing where it was going to go. I would write about an idea and insert it where I thought it would fit best. My second draft was an attempt to organize my thoughts so that they made sense. Then I sent it out to my village, still with some rough spots. This was not easy for me to do.

HABIT / I would light a candle before I started writing. It was my cue that helped me focus and kept me from getting distracted. I plan to buy a board game—an expensive one, too—when this book gets published as my reward. My routine has been to exercise, eat, shower, and then begin writing each morning, three days a week.

USEFUL / I ENJOY A GOOD MOVIE AND A GOOD VIDEO GAME. HOWEVER, I HAD TO LIMIT ALL MY DISTRACTIONS UNTIL THE WEEKEND TO HELP ME STAY FOCUSED AND PRODUCTIVE. I DID NOT PURCHASE ANY NEW BOARD OR VIDEO GAMES, KNOWING THEY COULD DISTRACT ME FROM MY WORK.

A PILGRAMAGE TO
CREATIVITY PRAYER

On our first day of class we
gather together and say a
prayer to prepare our hearts
and minds for the semester. I
hope you will make it your own
prayer as well.

Our Father in heaven, we submit our bodies, minds, and souls as we embark on a pilgrimage to hear the whispers of our lives and practice creative habits.

*Give us **charity** on our pilgrimage as we put aside our prejudices and keep from making quick judgments so that we may seek what is good and true.*

*Give us **humility** on our pilgrimage so that we can see our own faults and make the appropriate changes that can move us towards health and freedom.*

*Give us **wisdom** on our pilgrimage so that we may orient our hearts to receive the truth and make good, sound judgments.*

And finally, may we gain a better understanding of our role as image-bearers as we gather together in this classroom so that we may redeem the world one creative act at a time. [18]

AMEN.

MY
CREATIVITY
MINIFESTO

I will respond to the whispers of my life
and not allow them to be suffocated by the
pressures of everyday life.

I will capture all my ideas, knowing that if I don't,
they will be lost forever.

I will speak truthfully about myself and replace
false scripts with the truth.

I will develop the capacity to focus deeply by
managing my tasks and simplifying my life.

I will study and practice to help me become a
master of my talent and field.

I will participate in a community which provides
support, encouragement, and truth.

I will design my environment so that it will inspire
me to do extraordinary things.

I will not allow perfectionism, self-doubt, fear, busyness,
procrastination, or excuses to defeat me.

I will foster the habit of creativity with
triggers and rewards.

I will produce work that is both
meaningful and redemptive.

I will keep moving forward no matter how many
times I fall short. I will never quit because the
world needs my contributions.

BOOK STORE

Want to master the creative life? Here are some good reads to keep your creative journey going. Each one approaches the topic of creativity from a different perspective. Look over the list and listen to which ones are calling your name.

The Creative Brain by Nancy C. Andreasen

Art and Fear by David Bayles & Ted Orland

The Artist Way by Julia Cameron

Creativity: Flow and the Psychology of Discovery and Invention by Mihaly Csikszentmihaly

Make Space by Scott Doorley & Scott Witthoft

Drawing on the Right Side of the Brain by Betty Edwards

The Accidental Creative by Todd Henry

The Art of Innovation by Tom Kelley

The Cambridge Handbook of Creativity
by James Kaufman & Robert Sternberg

Bird by Bird by Anne Lamont

Imagine by Jonah Lehrer

Disciplined Dreaming by Josh Linkner

Orbiting the Giant Hairball by Gordon MacKenzie

The Creativity Book by Eric Maisel

A Whack on the Side of the Head by Roger Von Oech

Your Creative Power by Alex Osborn

Understanding Creativity by Jane Piirto

A Whole New Mind by Daniel Pink

Not a Box by Antoinette Portis

The War of Art by Steven Pressfield

The Dot by Peter Reynolds

Sparks of Genius by Robert & Michele Root-Bernstein

Explaining Creativity by R. Keith Sawyer

InGenius by Tina Seelig

Creativity in the Classroom by Alane Jordan Starko

The Creative Habit by Twyla Tharp

Living the Creative Life by Rice Freeman-Zachery

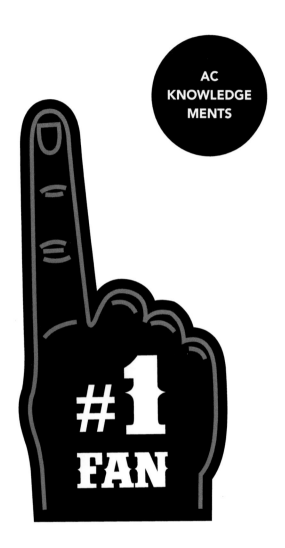

AC
KNOWLEDGE
MENTS

#1
FAN

FIRST / I acknowledge the contributions of Christian Smith. His work, *What is a Person?*, introduced the theory of emergence, which sparked the basic principle used in this book, creative emergence.

SECOND / I must acknowledge the many creativity pioneers, researchers, and practitioners who came before me. Without them this book would not have seen the light of day, nor would I have the immense pleasure of being a Professor of Creativity at a university. While I have never met most of them personally, I count each and every one of these people as my mentors and part of my village as they have taught me how to live a creative life.

THIRD / to my editor Andy McGuire. Thanks for cleaning up my mess.

I also want to thank a few individuals who played an important role in bringing about the IDS 101 Creativity, Innovation, and Problem Solving class, from which much of this book is based.

TIM DETWEILER / After a five minute conversation, you were convinced the creativity class should become a core requirement for all freshmen at Cornerstone University. Thanks for giving me a chance. Hey, I have another idea. Got five minutes?

JEANETTE BANASHAK, ELIZABETH WING, & DEBBIE HEWITT / My colleagues, friends, and heroes. Thanks for coming on board and teaching with me. Your wisdom and friendship is worth more than gold.

THE FIRST CREATIVITY CLASS / Thanks for being gracious and giving me a chance to fail often. Because of you, this material was born.

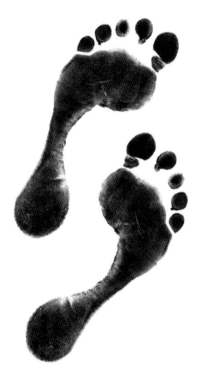

FOOT
NOTES

01 / You can read more about the Cultural Mandate in Nancy Pearcy's book, *Total Truth*.

02 / Culture-making is what we make of this world. It entails making gardens, books, languages, businesses, pictures, origami, cars, and everything in between.

03 / I have not copyrighted the term "blobism," nor do I have any desire to do so. You are free to use it as you please.

04 / Christian Smith's book, *What is a Person?*, has informed much of my thinking regarding the philosophical idea of emergence.

05 / The term "Creatives" has recently become popular and is used to denote creative people who practice the creative life or exercise creative habits.

06 / There is a great film about the creative life called Meet the Robinsons. The theme of the film is "keep moving forward," and you will see this phrase used several times throughout this book. The film makers bring to life one of Walt Disney's famous quotes, "Around here, however, we don't look backwards for very long. We keep moving forward, opening up new doors and doing new things, because we're curious...and curiosity keeps leading us down new paths."

07 / Nothing should ever replace the important task of parenting. One of the biggest problems our children face today is parents who consider their children "in the way." Parenting is hard and difficult, as you might already know. But our children should never take second fiddle. Setting aside time to do our creative endeavors can be difficult when trying to meet the needs of our children. I am still trying to find that balance.

08 / If we are to raise a generation of Creatives, students need to do more than memorize information and regurgitate facts. Students should study the habits of historical figures so they will discover the kind of life it takes to accomplish goals.

09 / While Creatives are involved in healthy villages, they also recognize the importance of working alone. In fact, most of our creative work is done in solitude.

10 / Catalyst Ranch website: *www.catalystranch.com*

11 / I also see another trend in our society. It is one where everyone is a winner. We believe that competition is bad and that we shouldn't keep score. This is just another pendulum swing. What our children need is both collaboration and competition, appropriate to their developmental level. Let's not raise one idea up at the expense of the other.

12 / This is just a random footnote. Made you look.[16]

13 / Dopamine addiction is very real and should not be dismissed. There are now centers that help people with their online addictions. If you or a loved one has a problem in this area, there is no shame in seeking help. In fact, it takes courage to do so. Be courageous.

14 / For more information regarding the National Survey of Youth and Religion, go to www.youthandreligion.org, or check out the book Lost In Transition by Christian Smith.

15 / Everything from social, to biological, to environmental, to technological factors influence human behavior and development. However, I also recognize that each person has a free will and is responsible for their own actions. The role of the Spirit is to transcend any types of determinism we have experienced and to enlighten us of our misunderstandings.

16 / I am just footnoting a footnote. This is new for me.[17]

17 / This is starting to be fun, and ridiculous, at the same time.

18 / I have used this reference before in my lectures and been accused of believing that humans, not God, redeem the world. So to clarify, I believe that God is the only one who can atone for our sins. But He uses broken individuals, like me, to make this world a better place through our creative acts.